The Colours of Yesterday's Trams

Martin Jenkins and Ian Stewart

Photo restoration by Michael Eyre

Capital Transport

Acknowledgements

The authors wish to thank Michael Eyre for his outstanding image restoration work; Barry 'Curly' Cross for his support and generosity; David L. Thomson for his meticulous checking of the manuscript; E.C. Bennett, A. Brotchie, P. Davey, G.G. Fairley, M. Greenwood, J.B. Horne, R.W.A. Jones, J. Kilroy, H. McAulay, A.D. Packer, G.W. Price, D.L. Thomson, G. Tilt, A. Watt and I. Yearsley for checking the captions; and finally all those who kindly provided introductions to most of the systems.

The authors also wish to thank Colour-Rail, the LCC Tramways Trust, London Transport Museum, the LRTA (London Area), the Manchester Tramway Museum Society, the National Tramway Museum, the National Geographic, the North-West Film Archive, Online Transport Archive, Seashore Trolley Museum and the Scottish Tramway & Transport Society.

In writing the captions, the authors referred to many publications too numerous to list but wish to express their gratitude to the many authors involved.

Martin Jenkins
Ian Stewart

Frontispiece This remarkable view of Renfield Street, Glasgow, was captured on Kodachrome film and published in *The National Geographic Magazine* in May 1946 a year after the photograph was taken. At this time Glasgow's route colour system was still being adhered to, not being finally abandoned until the early 1950s. Only the white cars had been eliminated (by 1942), hence red, green and yellow cars are prominent, and there is even a blue car at the top of the hill. There was no blue service using Renfield Street at this time, and it is thought that this must have been a depot transfer. One of the experimental 'Lightweight' cars also descends in the distance. However, it would come as a complete surprise to most Glaswegians to see a single-decker in town. Many would not know of their existence, as they were generally confined to service 20, which ran from Clydebank to Duntocher, miles to the west of this location. The car is No 975, and it is being driven by a fitter, presumably from its home depot at Partick, for attention at the Coplawhill Car Works, to the south of the city. Its presence by pure chance gives this view added rarity. The blackout restrictions were lifted in April 1945, and one tram can be seen with the white collision fenders already restored to maroon. Otherwise the wartime impositions are still evident, including blackout paint on the 'Coronation' tram's eaves glasses and the restricted destination displays (although all the screens remained *in situ*). Although the clock displays 2.10pm the UK had adopted double summer time during this period, and it must have been a warm day judging by the gabardine raincoats that are either unfastened or carried. Soldiers in uniform are also prominent. The white 'blemish' obscuring part of the red (service 25) tram is actually a disc suspended from span wire, indicating 'EP' (electric points) as a warning to motormen. The other warning to motormen was the traction pole with the large expanse of white paint, indicating the presence of a section insulator in the traction supply through which trams were to be driven without power applied. Further up the hill the *Paramount* Cinema had yet to be renamed the *Odeon*. Basically the scene is little changed today, although all the buildings have been stone-cleaned. *B. Anthony Stewart, courtesy* The National Geographic Magazine

First published 2012

ISBN 978-1-85414-356-3

Published by Capital Transport Publishing
www.capitaltransport.com

Printed by 1010 Printing International Ltd

Contents

Introduction

Below left Until recently it was impossible to imagine publishing colour views of trams in places like Bournemouth, a 3ft 6in gauge system which closed on 8 April 1936, but by freeze-framing images from period cine films it is now possible to study a remarkable scene like this, which shows two open-top bogie cars in their striking livery of chocolate and primrose. As with many other narrow-gauge systems, Board of Trade regulations governing operations on steep grades meant the town never had top-covered cars. Although popular in warm weather, open-toppers were hardly ideal in inclement conditions. Historically, Blackpool. Bournemouth and London, employed the conduit method of current collection in the UK. Until replaced by overhead wires in 1911 the conduit was used on all tracks within a half-mile radius of The Square. Between 1902 and 1926 various groups of open-top bogie cars entered service. On the right in this view is one from a batch of 20 delivered in 1921, whilst that on the left is one of 20 delivered during the period 1924-26. Built by the Brush Electrical Engineering Co, of Loughborough, these 68-seaters rode on Brill 22E maximum-traction bogies, the newer group coming complete with driver's windscreens. Looking so large on the narrow-gauge tracks, they were known locally as 'Dreadnoughts'. When the system closed in 1936, ten were sold to Llandudno and a number of traction motors to Liverpool Corporation. *North-West Film Archive*

This book has been an exciting and demanding challenge, and the authors are indebted to Capital Transport for its whole-hearted support and Michael Eyre for his many hours of work restoring images. Both authors began taking colour slides in the late 1950s and have over the years, collected images from many sources, including some from overseas. Having discovered ever more potential candidates, we came to realise we had a unique opportunity to bring together a comprehensive range of colour images which, when taken together, create a unique coverage of the tramway scene in the British Isles, especially from 1948 onwards.

Of course, the quality of many early images varies considerably. For example, we have included one of the legendary Newcastle F class purely for its rarity value. A few of our selected images have appeared in other publications but they help to complete the coverage of a particular system. With an increasing choice of images from the mid-1950s onwards we have been able to illustrate most car types in the major fleets.

At the end of the Second World War colour photography was still in its infancy; furthermore it was very expensive. Most shots were hand-held, taken at slow shutter speeds and with a lens whose aperture rarely exceeded f5.6. As a result there was sometimes a degree of 'motion blur' on moving vehicles.

The handful of UK photographers who had the foresight to create a colour record of the vanishing tramway scene in the early post-war years tended to be cautious, selecting where possible bright, open locations such as termini, where vehicles were also stationary. Colour photography was usually curtailed during dark or inclement weather. However, as film quality improved during the 1950s it became possible for the growing number of photographers working in colour to take ever better images. Some of the American visitors whose slides are seen in the book had superior cameras and better-quality lenses.

The images selected by the authors include bustling city centres, tramway hubs, a subway, steep gradients, narrow streets (sometimes with single track and loops), leafy suburbs, depots, reserved tracks and industrial, rural and seaside backdrops. The trams include pre-First World War survivors, war-weary veterans, 1930s 'streamline' double- and single-deckers, experimental one-offs, second-hand acquisitions, works cars, rebuilds and single- and double-deck cars built after the Second World War.

Below right The Second World War prolonged the life of many British tram systems. Abandonment programmes were postponed, some recently closed routes reopened and life-expired cars were kept on the road. Salford was very much a case in point. When the system closed at the end of March 1947 it was said to be in deplorable condition. The only known colour images are from a 1942 Road Safety film. This broadside view shows one of 12 Brush-built cars delivered during 1914-15 complete with canopy top cover and driver's vestibule. Riding on Brill 37E bogies, they were in virtually original condition when withdrawn during 1946-47. The Salford system once connected with several neighbouring tramways, including Manchester's, over which it had some running rights and at one time operated several joint services. *North-West Film Archive*

Historically, the first street horse-drawn tramway in Britain opened at Birkenhead in 1860. The first electric street tramway which used the conduit method of current collection was opened at Blackpool in 1885 and the first drawing power from an overhead wire at Leeds in 1891. Rapid conversion to electricity of horse, steam and cable-operated tramways followed together with the construction of many new systems but by the beginning of the First World War, the great programme of tramway expansion was almost over although the number of trams continued to grow reaching a peak of some 14,000 by the late 1920s.

The first full abandonment occurred at Sheerness as early as 1917. Wartime neglect coupled with rising costs and an increasing preference for buses and trolleybuses led to more systems closing during the 1920s. A major blow came with publication of a Royal Commission on Transport which condemned the tram as obsolete with the result that during the 1930s some 60 systems were totally abandoned and major cities such as Birmingham, Dublin, Manchester, London, Newcastle, Portsmouth, Plymouth, Salford etc were actively pursuing tram replacement programmes.

Those keeping faith with the tram included Aberdeen, Blackpool, Dundee, Edinburgh, Glasgow, Leeds, Liverpool, Sheffield and Sunderland, with many of these undertakings building new cars often in their own workshops. Even after the Second World War, new trams entered service in Aberdeen, Blackpool, Glasgow, Leeds and Sheffield.

Of systems closed during and immediately after the Second World War, no colour has come to light of trams in Coventry (1940); Southend (1942); Stalybridge, Hyde, Mossley & Dukinfield (1945); Hull, except for a former passenger car converted to a works car, 1945); Plymouth (1945); Bolton (1947) and Bessbrook and Newry (1947).

Partly through the evolving process of freeze-framing images from colour cine film it is possible to enjoy some remarkable images of trams operating in Bournemouth (closed 1936), Lytham St Annes (1937), Brighton (1939), Bristol (1941) and Salford (1947).

Most of the systems which survived the war were photographed in colour and, owing to the second-hand market, cars from abandoned systems could be recorded in their new homes and include vehicles from Accrington (abandoned 1931), Bury (1949), Darwen (1946), Huddersfield (1940), Oldham (1946), Portsmouth (1936), South Shields (1946) as well as Ilford.

By 1945 there were still some 6,200 trams, working on 40 richly varied systems. This book follows the closure of these systems in chronological order up to the abandonment of Glasgow in 1962 and the closure of the last of the non-Promenade routes in Blackpool in 1963, by which time fewer than 200 trams remained in the UK.

Of the systems surviving today, the authors have included only Blackpool with a selection of images taken before 1964 featuring withdrawn car types and the town routes closed in the early 1960s. The other survivors have altered very little over the past 50 years except, in some cases, for a considerable reduction in service.

Martin Jenkins and Ian Stewart

Below left The standard gauge (4ft 8¹/₂ in) Lytham St Annes system closed on 28 April 1937. It had operating rights into Blackpool and latterly Lytham trams reached as far north as The Gynn, where one of the original fleet of 30 four-wheel open-toppers is seen in 1935. This is probably the only known colour image of a car built entirely by the British Electric Car Co, of Trafford Park, Manchester. Most operators disposed of BEC-built cars because the bodies were of such inferior construction, but Lytham kept its examples on the road, most receiving various modifications.
North-West Film Archive

When the 4ft-gauge Accrington system closed in 1932 one of its fully-enclosed bogie cars was sent on trial to Lytham. Dating from 1915, the 76-seat Brush-built car was re-gauged and re-motored, but the all-weather crush-loader was not entirely successful, as its maximum-traction bogies kept derailing. As a result Lytham decided not to purchase three similar cars from Accrington. Seen at The Gynn in its eye-catching bright blue and cream livery, 55 was nicknamed 'Big Bertha' or 'Waltzing Matilda'. In the background is one of the new generation of Blackpool 'Railcoaches', while just visible on the right is one of the 'Pantograph' cars in its mid-1930s livery.
North-West Film Archive

Left and centre With gradients as steep as 1 in 9, Brighton adopted the 3ft 6in narrow gauge and operated only open-top four-wheel cars. From 1914 the Corporation built its own 52-seater bodies, and eventually the entire fleet was mounted on Brill 21E trucks. These two views were recorded in the spring of 1939. In the first, No 77 is at the Aquarium, focal point of the 10-mile system. This was one of 13 Class E cars dating from the period 1929-31 and is in the lined-out version of the brick-red and cream livery. The headlamps are positioned above the destination displays, and route letters are carried on the side of the upper-deck railings. There were also wooden route boards beneath the lower deck windows. The second view features one of the many cars to receive replacement bodies, the last 31 Class F cars having a more pleasing style with shallower windscreens. The body on No 52 saw service only from 1937 to 1939. Here it is in the final simplified livery. The system closed on 31 August 1939. *Courtesy Leeds Transport Historical Society (photographer unknown)*

Bottom Only Bristol and Coventry closed as a direct result of enemy action during the Second World War, Bristol closing on 11 April 1941. Among the 8,000 trams still operating in 1939 those at Bristol looked decidedly old-fashioned. Although reluctant to invest in new vehicles in case of a Corporation takeover, the tramways company did rebuild the majority of its 53-seat cars to a standard design, one of which is seen with driver Dick Dawe at Westbury a year after the Corporation takeover in 1937. Built by G. F. Milnes & Co in 1900, No 5 had a Peckham cantilever truck of 6ft 6in wheelbase, and two 28hp motors. It is in the final livery of dark blue and white. The car was broken up in 1941. *S. Miles Davey*

Above right An early G. F. Milnes car at the Tramways Centre. The staircases, Tudor-arch windows and metal lifeguards all emphasise the elderly design. The wooden route boards were fitted into slots outside the lower-deck windows. No 66 was broken up in 1939, the year after the Corporation decided to replace the trams. *Courtesy Peter Davey (photographer unknown)*

Right This remarkable view of the four-track layout at Old Market Street was recorded at 2.30pm on 3 June 1939 by local photographer and historian Reece Winstone. After reversing, the Milnes car in the foreground will travel along the Kingswood route as far as Whiteway Road. Behind it is one of 20 cars imported from the USA in 1898. Built by the American Car Co, these had rounded tops to the windows and larger ventilator slots. No 143 still carries the old company title. In the background is the *Empire Theatre*. On Good Friday 1941 the power supply was severely damaged during an air-raid, and tramway operation ended abruptly, the remaining 40 or so trams being scrapped shortly afterwards. *Reece Winstone Archive*

MANCHESTER

STANDARD GAUGE, CLOSED 9 JANUARY 1949

A city with overhead wires seemingly etched into the sky above every main street, this was the Manchester where trams were splashes of colour against the grimy backdrop of buildings encrusted with the soot of coal fires and factory chimneys beyond all counting. Howard Spring in his novels saw the night-time trams as galleons of light, Adolphe Valette celebrated them with oil paint and canvas on misty days. But there was a range of liveries, for eight other operators entered the city, and the vermillion and cream of Manchester and Salford met a spectrum of colours right through to the blue, white and red of Ashton or the dark hedge green of the Stalybridge joint board. Yet few attained the gaudy (latterly dingy) magnificence of the Manchester livery — or the complexity of its route-numbering system. Down-to-earth and cosmopolitan, the city bred people who rode their trams with pride.

Ian Yearsley

The city's big six-window bogie cars were renowned for their wrought iron work, coloured quarter lights, elaborate lining-out and maximum-traction bogies. After London and Glasgow this was the third-largest tramway in Britain, with just over 950 cars operating on 123 route miles. It was also the centre of a vast network of inter-connected systems with through running and joint services. Although new cars were built until 1932 the first tram-to-bus conversion occurred two years earlier. This image taken from a pre-war cine film shows, 822, one of the city's first totally-enclosed bogie cars at Ardwick Green. Built in 1920 by English Electric, it had a flat roof, curved ends that were narrower than the upper-deck panels, deeper lower-deck windows and outside indicator boxes. With seats for 78 passengers and riding on 22E type bogies, it was withdrawn in 1939. Note the skate in the overhead which enabled cars to operate the automatic points at the approaching junction. *North-West Film Archive*

Between 1924 and 1930, 110 'Replacement cars' emerged from Hyde Road works. Built to the same general design as the bogie cars, they were technically rebuilds of older two-axle vehicles and rode on Manchester's version of the 22E bogie. Looking spick and span, No 434 was filmed at Ardwick Green probably prior to July 1937 when the former jointly-operated route 34 was divided into its Salford part and its Manchester part. This was one of the 'Replacement cars' to have a curved as opposed to a flat roof and large as opposed to small lower deck windows. It lasted through the war and was withdrawn shortly afterwards. The red band painted on the traction pole (left) indicated a bus stop; the tram stops having a white band above he top of the red band and the collar. *North West Film Archive*

Further batches of high-capacity bogie cars entered service during the 1920s with the last 50 being delivered during 1927-28. Originally, these English Electric-built cars with their curved roofs, upper-deck panels flush with the ends and built-in indicator boxes had seats for 80 passengers but this was later reduced to 76 with the fitting of transverse leather seating downstairs. One of the class, 1052, is seen crossing Belmont Bridge on Wellington Road North on service 35. Operated jointly with Stockport Corporation, this long route passed through two counties on its journey from Central Manchester to Hazel Grove. *Maurice Marshall collection, courtesy Manchester Transport Museum Society*

Manchester's tramway-replacement programme should have been completed in the early 1940s, but the war intervened, and the final routes were not abandoned until 1949. As a result Jack Batty was able to take this precious colour photograph of 960 in early January 1949. It came from a batch 60 English Electric built cars delivered during 1924-25. By the end, some 35 trams remained from the post-war total of 360. 960 is at Hazel Grove, the southernmost point of the once vast Manchester-area network of inter-connected tram systems. Stockport trams continued to serve Hazel Grove for another a year. *Jack Batty / Online Transport Archive*

DUBLIN

5FT 3IN GAUGE, CLOSED 9 JULY 1949

My father was a reporter, and towards the end of tram operation in July 1949 he took me with him to interview the crew of one of the last cars. I remember standing on the front platform as a burly motorman, swaying from side to side at the controls, spoke in a broad Dublin accent while my dad took notes in his little book. We then went upstairs to the open balcony above the platform and continued our journey to the seaport of Dalkey. I was fascinated by the swinging of the trolley boom as it trailed along the overhead cable, while the tram swayed gently from side to side as it clanked along. From the vantage-point of the balcony I could see oncoming trams from a great distance and was held spellbound as they glided graciously along the cobbled streets, the hissing of the overhead cable reminding me of sausages sizzling in a pan, and the occasional shower of sparks presented a magical spectacle to an imaginative child.

Jim Kilroy

Few colour photographs exist of trams in Dublin, which at its peak had some 330 cars. Here 199 leaves O'Connell Bridge bound for Dartry, a route abandoned in 1948. This was one of 58 'Standard Saloons' built by Dublin United Tramways (DUT) between 1924 and 1929 and mounted on Brill 21E trucks. Visible in the background is the statue of Daniel O'Connell and the former six-track hub flanking Nelson Pillar. Many of the buses are on tram-replacement services. Modern LUAS trams now cross O'Connell Street at right angles. *W. E. Robertson, courtesy Martin Jenkins / Online Transport Archive*

This atmospheric scene, unearthed by J. M. Canfield, was recorded in 1946 by an American visitor to Dublin. Although not a transport enthusiast, his photograph shows the final terminal arrangements on the west side of the O'Connell monument. Both cars are bound for Dalkey, this being the last route to close. The first is open-balcony bogie car 231, whilst the second, 132, is from a batch of 37 60-seat 'Luxury' trams built by DUT between 1932 and 1936 and mounted on Maley & Taunton swing-link trucks. Along with two other cars, 132 was the subject of an early preservation scheme which, unfortunately, failed. *J. M. Canfield collection / Online Transport Archive*

BLACKBURN

4FT GAUGE, CLOSED 3 SEPTEMBER 1949

There can't be very many active enthusiasts around who actually rode and photographed Blackburn trams. As a young schoolboy I did so twice, on both occasions accompanying the legendary Bob Parr. The visits were worthwhile, for Blackburn cars offered a smart (but well-scrubbed) dark green livery and a superb ride on their Peckham 14B bogies. A few cars remained with open tops. On most cars the steel underframes were not cantilevered for the platforms, so it was a climb to board. The cars looked a bit 'different'. Were the bodies built in Germany under sub-contract from Milnes? The route scene ranged from close-packed workers' houses to open moorland.

David Packer

Opposite and Above After taking his first colour view in 1939, the late Clarence Carter then took an extraordinary range of colour images during the 1940s and 1950s. During a visit to Blackburn on 20 August 1949 he recorded several views of the final route which was itself the last remnant of a network of inter-connected 4ft-gauge tramways that once served north-east Lancashire. The elderly trams had started life in 1901 as G. F. Milnes open-top, open-fronted bogie cars but during the 1920s were rebuilt by the Corporation as fully-enclosed cars able to pass under low bridges; this was achieved by reconstructing the original Peckham 14B bogies and fitting smaller wheels and motors. In the first view 41, in its faded sage green and cream livery, is at the kerbside loading point in Salford in the centre of Blackburn whilst in the second, No 39 is at Intack. Until 1932 Accrington trams passed through here on a jointly-operated service between the two towns; then from 1932 until 1949, Blackburn trams continued beyond Intack to Church. *C. Carter / Online Transport Archive*

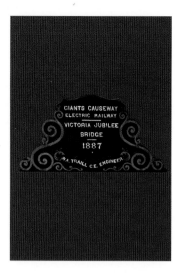

GIANT'S CAUSEWAY

3ft GAUGE, CLOSED 30 SEPTEMBER 1949

The Giant's Causeway, Portrush and Bush Valley Railway and Tramway Company's line opened to the public on 29 January 1883. Steam tram locomotives were used until electrification in September of that year when it became the first electrically-powered line in the United Kingdom. Power was generated hydroelectrically, the steam locos being retained into the 1920s for back up and tourist traffic. Originally the power supply was third rail which proved somewhat hazardous, the line being a mix of street, roadside and cross-country, and it was converted to overhead in 1899. The scenic 7½-mile line carried passengers to within a mile of the famous stone columns at the Giant's Causeway. Notoriously slow, its speed of about 7mph features in a song about the line by the group The Irish Rovers.

Opposite This three car train is waiting to leave the outer terminus to return to Portrush in July 1949. Mounted on a Peckham truck and powered by 2 x 20hp motors, 9 was one of the tramway's six motor cars and may have started life as a trailer built by the Midland Railway Carriage and Wagon Works. Also on view are two of nine toastrack trailers, some of which started life without canopy covers. *AD Hutchinson*

Above The line had several unusual operating practices. During summer peaks, when five three-car trains were used, the approach to some loops was blind so boys armed with flags stood above the track at key vantage points in order to signal drivers through the loops. Waiting to proceed to Portrush in July 1949 is one of four former open toast-rack motor cars. At the rear is one of three closed trailers with platform ends. To save on electricity, cars often freewheeled into Portrush with their trolleys tied down for the final descent. This historic line with its breath-taking views of the Atlantic Ocean last ran on 30 September 1949. All attempts to have it re-opened have failed. *AD Hutchinson*

LEICESTER

STANDARD GAUGE, CLOSED 9 NOVEMBER 1949

There were easy ways to explore this system. One was to board either a 1 or a 2 at the Clock Tower and stay on until it returned there for the third time! The Clock Tower was the hub and a tram could cross from any one of four streets to any other. I first watched trams negotiating these various junctions on 14 July 1945. Later, I boarded car 133 on service 4, which had single line and loops in Clarendon Park Road. At Aylestone Road junction I boarded car 55 for a run down to Horsefair Street and followed this with rides on 68 and 141 around the Blackbird Road / Abbey Road circle. Riding Leicester's trams, with their wooden seats and maple ceilings in the lower saloon, took one back to the 1930s, although 141 did have upholstered 2+1 seating.

Richard Wiseman

This was a fairly conventional city system with a compact network of routes much of which survived the Second World War. Latterly the 160 or so four-wheel cars bore a strong family resemblance, the last examples being delivered in 1920. No 68 (which Richard Wiseman rode in 1945) was from a group of 99 open-top trams built by Dick, Kerr & Co and mounted on Brill 21E trucks. Successive upgrades finally transformed them into totally-enclosed cars between 1924 and 1932, except for six cars which were withdrawn after the first abandonment, Melbourne Road on 13th December 1933. More powerful motors were also fitted and, in most cases, improved controllers. When Clarence Carter visited the city on 15 May 1949 he took a handful of colour images including this view of No 68 in Evington Road on the East Park Road route. The car retains its reversed stairs and wooden longitudinal seating in the lower saloon. Those still in this pre-1937 livery were known locally as 'ice cream carts'. *C. Carter*

Dating from 1905 and seen here in final condition, 102 was one of 20 top-covered open-balcony cars built by the United Electric Car Co. On 15 May 1949 the driver prepares to release the handbrake as it makes its way to East Park Road via London Road. This livery was first introduced in 1937. Note the route number located in the vestibule.
C. Carter / Online Transport Archive

A total of 23 cars, including 138 seen here in Victoria Park Road, were given new frames and extended platforms during the period 1931 to 1937, while 14 cars, again including 138, were fitted with comfortable transverse upholstered leather seats in the lower saloon between April 1932 and March 1935. Dating from 1905 and seen here in final condition, 102 was one of 20 top-covered open-balcony cars built by the United Electric Car Co. On 15 May 1949 the driver prepares to release the handbrake as it makes its way to Clarendon Park via London Road. This livery was first introduced in 1937. Note the boarding instructions on the platform step – this was an attempt to speed up movements at busy stops.
C. Carter / Online Transport Archive

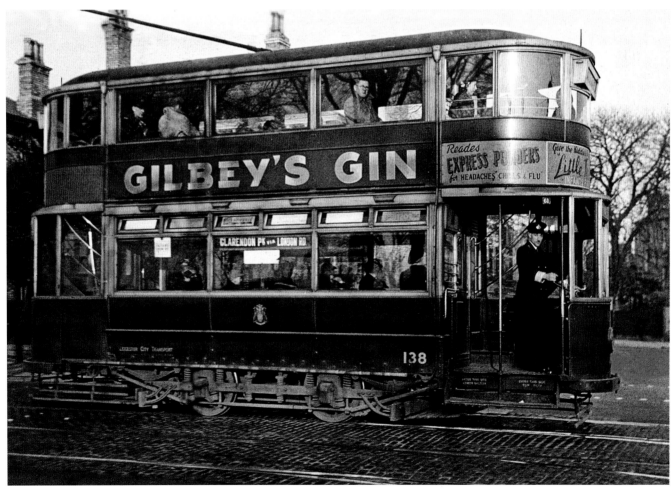

ROTHERHAM

STANDARD GAUGE, CLOSED 13 NOVEMBER 1949

My first ride on a Rotherham car came on 27 November 1948. I waited at the long dismal shelter in the centre of town and boarded No 5, one of the single-enders. Upstairs, I took my place on the right hand comfortable double seat. Once on the move it was like sitting in the front of a modern trolleybus except for the smoothness of the acceleration. Once on the main Sheffield road, we crossed the River Rother at Ickles Bridge before entering the industrial heartland of the Don Valley. Just beyond the bridge is the crossover used by two older, double-ended cars at rush hours. We travelled along the busy road lined with steelworks and factories, passed under three railway bridges, the reversing triangle at Temple Street, the Sheffield boundary sign and then I crossed over Tinsley Bridge for the last time. It closed a fortnight later, and Rotherham's trams were cut back to Templeborough.

Richard Wiseman

Opposite Local politics kept trams remaining on one route for longer than expected. Although most of the system had been converted to trolleybus operation Sheffield Corporation refused to consider introducing trolleybuses onto the joint service between the two towns. As a result Rotherham invested in 11 new vehicles, which entered service during 1934-35. With loops at either end of the line, the English Electric bodies were unidirectional with one entrance, one staircase and 63 fixed seats. They rode on EMB flexible-axle trucks. After the war Rotherham costed a rehabilitation programme. However, when the joint service was suspended in 1948 for a bridge-replacement project Sheffield opted for bus replacement, so for the last 11 months the single-enders operated only within the Rotherham boundary. Shortly before the end a dismal-looking No 4 is seen in the town centre. *C. Carter / Online Transport Archive*

Above Still looking quite respectable, No 9 is on the reversing stub at Templeborough ('Templebro' on blinds). To undertake reversals and back-up manoeuvres these unique cars had controls and brakes at the rear as well as small headlights. In the background is the main Rotherham–Sheffield road which in those days was flanked by giant steelworks, factories and industrial plant. *C. Carter / Online Transport Archive*

19

SOUTHAMPTON

STANDARD GAUGE, CLOSED 31 DECEMBER 1949

Oh to ride again through Southampton streets on an open-top tram in the sunshine! Wonderful ancient cars mingled with smart domed-roof ones on a system whose routes were more complicated than you could imagine — it was possible to take a trip from Docks, Royal Pier or Floating Bridge and up through the town by various inter-linking routes and return a quite different way! The domed roofs had fitted under the historic Bargate, but there were open-top trams with knifeboard seating and other elderly cars on which you could still see, on the trucks, the bolt-holes where London had fitted conduit gear before selling the cars to Southampton during the First World War. Few tramways had quite the magic of Southampton.

Barry Cross

Ingenuity was required in this busy south coast port to ensure trams were able to pass through the Bargate, a low medieval arch. At first, special low-height cars with knifeboard seating on the top deck were used. Passengers sat in the middle of the upper deck facing out rather than at the sides facing forward when passing through the arch. Then the general manager, James Dobson designed five open-toppers to pass through the arch. Entering service during 1920-25, these had lower bodies which allowed for transverse seats on the upper deck, smaller wheels and high speed motors. Later, manager Percy Baker devised their turtle roofs which turned Dobson's design into the 'Top-covered Bargate' type of which No 8 is seen boarding passengers in Commercial Road in 1949. After withdrawal this car was scrapped in Southampton, but at the time of writing car 11 from this pioneering batch is being restored by the Tram 57 Group. *W. E. Robertson / Colour-Rail IR367*

To operate fully-enclosed double-deckers through the Bargate, Manager Percy Baker lowered the track and designed a low-height body to be mounted on a truck with small wheels and high-speed motors. Between 1923 and 1931 some 55 cars with distinctive contoured roofs emerged from Portswood Works. Most were new, but some were rebuilds of older cars. No 19 was one of a batch of eleven 70-seaters built between 1923 and 1929. Although most of the system survived the war, the decision had already been taken to scrap the trams. Fortunately American enthusiast, Bill Robertson, took a few colour slides of the last route in October 1949. In this scene, 19 is about to turn from the High Street into Bernard Street. On the left is a pre-war Rover, and on the right an ex-military Hillman Utility still with its canvas back and spare tyre on the roof. Also visible are the Bargate, the Dolphin Hotel and the bomb-damaged Holy Rood Church, as well as a man cleaning windows (sadly not George Formby!). Although sold to Leeds this car never re-entered service, its body ending up on a pig farm.
W. E. Robertson / Colour-Rail IR369

At Floating Bridge passengers transferred to and from a chain ferry which until 1977 crossed the River Itchen. Seen here is one of the 12 'Pullman' versions of the domed-roof cars. Built between 1929 and 1931, these vehicles had curved flush sides, upholstered 2+2 seating on both decks, Peckham P35 trucks, two 40hp motors and air brakes (removed during the war). The livery was officially dark red and cream. During the war, several cars had their upper decks painted grey and some were grey all over. The 'Pullmans' were all sold to Leeds.
W. E. Robertson / Colour-Rail IR371

CARDIFF

STANDARD GAUGE, CLOSED 20 FEBRUARY 1950

Living in Grangetown, we had a choice of tram to go to town. My favourite was the 7 single-deck service to the splendid-sounding Roath Splott. Climbing aboard the tram, which looks majestic in its maroon and cream livery, we are immediately aware of the large spacious platforms where one can stand and watch the driver. We slow down for the single track over the Taff Bridge and, if we are lucky, will see moored at the Pumping Station an iron ship which has brought coal for the station's boilers. We progress under a low railway bridge taking the Taff Vale railway line to Clarence Road and then along another single track section before the steep incline to the Monument. In the city we pass through the centre of the fruit-and-vegetable district, where horse-drawn drays await custom. At one point we see a crossover intended for the proposed express service from the east of the city, destined never to be introduced.

R. W. A. Jones

The Welsh capital had a compact, all-street-track system and between 1923 and 1925 took delivery of 81 low-height 64-seat Brush-built double-deckers. Designed to pass under low railway bridges these cars had well-type underframes and Peckham P22 trucks with small wheels and motors. Similar cars were purchased by other operators. No 80 is seen here shortly after delivery in its livery of crimson lake and cream.
'The Open-Road' (1926), Claude Freise-Greene.

Conversion to trolleybuses began in 1942 and just under a year before the final closure, Clarence Carter took a few precious colour views on 9 March 1949 including this one of No 92 at Whitchurch Road.
C. Carter / Online Transport Archive

This is probably the only known colour view showing a car in wartime grey livery. Furthermore, 114 (left) still has its fender painted white, although the wartime headlamp mask has been removed. Both cars display Pay As You Enter (PAYE) notices. Under this system, which lasted from 1942 to 1950, tickets were dispensed with, even though vehicles remained two-man. After depositing their money in a glass-sided box passengers travelled any distance for 1d. The only Cardiff tram to be preserved is water car 131, now part of the National Tramway collection at Crich in Derbyshire. *C. Carter / Online Transport Archive*

NEWCASTLE

STANDARD GAUGE, CLOSED 4 MARCH 1950

In 1946, before complete conversion to rubber-tyred public transport, Byker passengers could travel over their surviving Raby Street route on a Class B tram for a halfpenny. This was a useful economy for an impecunious engineering apprentice enjoying a short introduction to the Newcastle system and still able to venture to Gosforth, Scotswood, along Jesmond Road and through Shieldfield. Several years later I witnessed nightly victims for execution processing from Byker depot via West Moor to Gosforth Park. My final experience was a ride on Newcastle's final car from Gateshead's Wrekenton terminus to Byker, which arrived at its destination early on 5 March 1950.

Tony Wickens

By 1939 Newcastle had a fleet of some 100 trolleybuses operating in part over routes taken over from trams. After the war, the abandonment programme was resumed. Colour views are scarce, but, inspired by his photographer father, a young Derek Charlton took a handful of colour images in order to capture 'the magnificent livery of dark maroon and cadmium yellow'. Although not sharp, the rarest, dating from 1946, depicts one of the much-rebuilt 'F'-class cars. These had started life in 1901 as open-sided, rear-loading single-deckers built by Hurst Nelson and mounted on Brill 27G equal-wheel bogies. Eventually they were rebuilt by the Corporation into massive double-deckers. Later modifications ensured no two were exactly alike. No 108 was one of the three highest capacity trams in the UK. Officially it carried 147 (92 seats), but local expert George Hearse recalls seeing up to 200 on board — no wonder there were early notices warning passengers to 'beware pickpockets'. This giant crowd-mover has a top cover, an extended upper deck, lengthened platforms and was latterly powered by just one motor per bogie.
D. G. Charlton / Colour-Rail IR362

This was one of 22 'G'-class open-toppers built by the Corporation in 1904-5 and rebuilt in the late 1920s as enclosed cars. The straight staircases installed at this time are clearly visible in this view of 172 taken in Stephenson Road probably in 1948. *D. G. Charlton*

Between 1917 and 1920 the Corporation built five fully-enclosed cars, and these were followed in 1921-26 by 70 Brush-built Class B fully-enclosed 62-seaters on Peckham P22 trucks. These five-window trams had straight staircases for the rear-entrance, front-exit arrangement. Before doors were fitted, draughts whistled up one flight of stairs and down the other, chilling all those on the upper deck. On 17 May 1949 car 240 waits to leave Central station for Scotswood Bridge. *C. Carter / Online Transport Archive*

The 55-seat, open-balcony 'E'-class cars were built variously by Brush and the Corporation between 1912 and 1918. Outside Newcastle Central station on 13 September 1949 three workmen clamber onto Brush-built 220, working one of the routes operated jointly with the Gateshead & District Tramways Co. To speed up passenger movements both operators had a substantial number of rear-entrance/front-exit cars. *C. Carter / Online Transport Archive*

In 1948 three much-rebuilt Class C single-deckers of 1901 were sold to the Grimsby & Immingham Electric Railway. Built by Hurst Nelson, they were among 25 of this class later fitted with Peckham P25 maximum-traction bogies and improved motors. In 1932-33 six, including those sold subsequently to the G&I, were 'Pullmanised' with 40 seats occupying two (instead of three) compartments. The clerestory roofing was also downswept over the platforms. The trio's sojourn on the G&I proved short. *Ray DeGroote / Online Transport Archive*

BRADFORD

4FT GAUGE, CLOSED 6 MAY 1950

Leaving St Mary's church at the top of Church Bank, my brother and I boarded a tram and sat on the open balcony at the front of the car. I recall being rather alarmed as the tram hurtled down the slope into Forster Square, jigging from side to side until it reached the bottom of the hill. I attribute my lifelong fear of heights to this one journey! Later, travelling with my father up Wakefield Road, I asked him why the tram clanked so much. "Naughty boys put pennies on the line," he explained. I clearly remember thinking "What a waste of a penny!"

Philip Hanson

Right Between 1919 and 1931, the Corporation built 96 62-seat 'Standard' cars most of which had 7ft-wheelbase trucks supplied by English Electric. Some 40 'Standards' survived to the end, among them 102, photographed at Odsal Top on 15 April 1950. The light blue livery dated from 1942. *J. Copland*

Opposite This was the last 4ft-gauge tramway in the country. Tram routes were already giving way to buses and trolleybuses when the war intervened. As a result, the replacement programme was officially suspended but some routes were abandoned due to the poor state of the infrastructure. The preponderance of steep gradients did not allow for the use of totally-enclosed cars so the 90 cars left after the war were balcony double-deckers. Seen at Queensbury on 19 May 1949, 107 was the sole survivor of a batch of ten 'High Top' four-window cars built by the Corporation in 1920. Mounted on a Boving truck, it lasted until the end of the year. *C. Carter / Online Transport Archive*

Following the last rites the body of 'Standard' 104 became a scoreboard at Odsal Stadium. Later it was rescued by local enthusiasts and, with considerable help from the Transport Department, restored to its former glory and painted in the pre-war livery of Prussian blue and white. Starting in July 1958, it occasionally operated on track approaching Thornbury Works, power being drawn from the trolleybus overhead. This unique operation ceased in the early 1960s, and since 1975 No 104 has been at a local industrial museum. *Phil Tatt / Online Transport Archive*

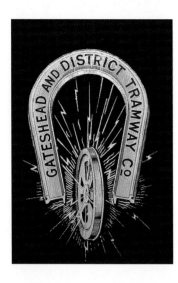

GATESHEAD

STANDARD GAUGE, CLOSED 4 AUGUST 1951

Almost until closure the Gateshead system, the last subsidiary of the British Electric Traction Company (BET), was well maintained, the smartly-turned-out trams contrasting with the drab, run-down Newcastle cars which inter-worked on four of their seven routes. The lines to Bensham and Wrekenton featured considerable gradients, six routes served terraced and inter-war Corporation housing, as did the Low Fell route, plus the middle-class 'semis' of Durham Road. The Heworth route passed into the Urban District of Felling to reach Heworth Church, now alongside the Heworth Interchange. By contrast the Wrekenton trams climbed steadily all the way from the Tyne Bridge to their mining village terminus, crossing a colliery railway *en route*. An enduring memory of the high-floored lengthy single-deckers is sitting in the middle and looking down at the tracks on certain very tight curves.

Hugh McAulay

Even after Newcastle's trams had gone, Gateshead cars continued running into the city over the High Level Bridge to a terminal point in Neville Street, at the eastern end of Newcastle Central station, where there had once been a four-track layout (note the severed curved track in the foreground). After the introduction of joint services in 1923 five points in Newcastle were linked with six termini in Gateshead but, by the time this photograph was taken in September 1950, this was the only terminus remaining in Newcastle. At the rear of this busy line up is Brush-built 'Standard' No 4 on the Low Fell route, while the ex-Oldham car is bound for Saltwell Park. Cars on two other routes — Dunston and Bensham — also reversed at this busy location. *C. Carter / Online Transport Archive*

Single-deckers
Surprisingly, for a system abandoned some 60 years ago, a number of colour images have survived thanks to, among others, Clarence Carter (again), Ian Davidson and Derek Charlton. Amazingly, some quality slides also surfaced recently at a transport flea-market. Together they help to illustrate the range and variety of this company fleet, which in 1945 included 35 single-deckers, the majority of which were 43ft-long bogie cars powered by two 50hp motors and fitted with longitudinal seats for 48 which allowed additional space for peak-time standees. The oldest survivors were the much-rebuilt G. F. Milnes cars 46-50 of 1902, which had started life as combination cars with semi-open-ended compartments (for smokers). The latter were enclosed in 1907; then, in the early 1930s, vestibules, longer platforms, doors for front-exit working, fixed windows and air brakes were fitted. No 46 is seen at Low Fell terminus. *I. Davidson / Colour-Rail IR348*

Low Fell terminus again this time with car 56 in about 1950. Dating from 1921, this was one of five Brush-built cars equipped with reversed maximum-traction Brill 39E bogies. Owing to a number of steep hills, cars had slipper brakes and, in most cases, air brakes. The incorporation of the destination indicator into the vestibule allows the 'Shop at Binns' enamelled plate to be displayed. When the hinged front exit door was opened a flag shot out warning other road users to 'STOP'. At night a light also came on to illuminate the disembarking passengers. *John Carlson collection*

With grimy Gateshead East station forming the backdrop, 13 is in Wellington Street. Shortly it will pass under the low bridge which had limited single-deck operation only to the Bensham, Dunston, Low Fell and Teams routes. In readiness for the introduction of joint services with Newcastle the company built several cars, including 13 and 15 which dated from 1920-21. These open platform cars had Brill 22E bogies, 10-window saloons, arched roofs (entirely hidden by advertising boards), ruby glass ventilators and opening quarterlights and, after 1926-27, vestibules and front exit doors. *John Carlson collection*

Between 1923 and 1928 a total of 16 'Standards' entered service of which two were built by Brush and the remainder — including No 5, seen here — by the company. All had eight windows, Brill 39E bogies and large-diameter (32in) wheels which required the floor level to be raised to provide clearance (in complete contrast to today's requirement for low floors and accessibility for the disabled). The restricted width of the destination indicator on this and other cars resulted in rather cramped displays such as 'Central Stn' in which the abbreviation was often highlighted in red. Seen at Low Fell, the car is devoid of all advertising, suggesting contracts had expired and were not being renewed. This was one of 19 cars sold to British Railways for use on the Grimsby & Immingham Electric Railway in 1951. Renumbered 20, it was ultimately acquired for the National Tramway Museum when the line closed in 1961. *John Carlson collection*

Double-deckers
Over the years, the Company purchased 30 new double-deckers for the Heworth, Saltwell Park and Wrekenton routes. After the war, the oldest survivors were 13 former open-toppers dating from 1901, all of which were rebuilt in the mid-1920s as vestibuled balcony cars with six windows per deck and 180° spiral staircases. Still on its original Brill 21E truck and powered by two 35hp motors, 32 is seen at Heworth on 17 May 1949. When this route was replaced by buses in March 1950 most balcony cars were withdrawn, although in rush hours trams still served Heworth for several more months. Nowadays. Heworth Metro Interchange is close to this location. *C. Carter*

Seven fully-enclosed, Brush-built 70-seaters were delivered in 1923. These had Brill 21E trucks (of 7ft 6in wheelbase), air brakes, two 50hp motors and 33in-diameter wheels. Their front exits were somewhat constrained by the close proximity of the adjacent curved stairs, and, in many ways, these cars were the equivalent of Newcastle's 'B' class, although the straight stairs in the latter avoided this problem. Car 67 is seen at Saltwell Park shortly before this route closed in March 1951 after which all double-deckers were withdrawn. The BET insignia comprising a magnet and a wheel can be seen above the destination indicator as well as the advertising along the rocker panel — a Gateshead feature. *I. Davidson*

Second hand cars

Above left The early 1920s saw the acquisition of eleven car bodies — three from Liverpool and eight from Sheffield. On arrival all received trucks and electrical equipment from withdrawn Company cars. Star of this remarkable 1946 streetscape is one of the ex-Sheffield cars which, during 1925-26, were rebuilt as balcony cars with platform vestibules but retaining their lower-deck 'Tudor arch' windows. Having started life in 1899, 37 is seen at the foot of High Street, an area once notorious for its many pubs. It is carrying a short-working slipboard in the driver's window. This view illustrates rather well the Gateshead livery, with straw-coloured lining-out, and confirms that the 'crimson' (tending towards brown) was nothing like the dark red worn by the buses of sister BET company Northern General. The car emerging from under the railway bridge is still in wartime grey-green. *D. Charlton / Colour-Rail 617*

Above right Six fully-enclosed cars purchased from Oldham in 1946 had Preston 21E trucks and two 40hp motors. Three dated from 1924, and one of these, 35 (the third bearer of that number in Gateshead), is seen on Barras Bridge, Newcastle, about to turn into the Museum terminus, described on Gateshead trams as 'Haymarket'. The date is 4 March 1950. This was the final day of joint Gateshead/Newcastle operation and also of joint tramway operation anywhere in the UK. Stretching into the distance are the de-wired tracks to Jesmond and Gosforth, now served by trolleybuses. *i. Davidson / Colour-Rail IR420*

Bottom left Ex-Oldham cars 68-70 of 1926 offered the comfort of leather-upholstered seating for 62 passengers. No 68 waits to leave Haymarket for the long run to Wrekenton. Note the use of the curved glass and the upper glazed panel of the top-deck front window, which in Oldham had incorporated a large route-number indicator. *D. Charlton / Colour-Rail IR618*

Bottom right In 1948 a mixed group of five single-deckers were acquired from Newcastle. Numbered 73-77 by their new owner, they had been built by Hurst Nelson in 1901 but were much altered over the years. For example, 77 was one of 25 'C'-class cars rebuilt in the 1920s for through running with Gateshead, being equipped with Peckham P25 maximum-traction bogies and two 40hp motors. Seen heading for Teams in March 1951, it also had air brakes, separate end smoking compartments and upholstered seats for 38. *I. Davidson / Colour-Rail IR425*

STOCKPORT

STANDARD GAUGE, CLOSED 25 AUGUST 1951

Had Stockport been in Spain or Italy, tourists would have flocked to admire its streets and alleys on many levels, its dramatic views of river, cliff-side and glimpses of moorland. In years past they could have seen tram routes crossing one above another, and a street where a power station's cooling tower offered intermittent rain. Latterly this Cheshire town provided the last vestige of the tramway networks of south-east Lancashire, its brightly painted cars providing a reproach to the increasing griminess of those in neighbouring cities.

Ian Yearsley

This was the last outpost of the once extensive network of tramways in the Manchester area. At its peak the 14¹/₂-mile system was worked by some 85 cars, and, in contrast to Manchester, these were well maintained to the end. Also some track was re-laid after the war. Wherever possible the Corporation standardised on trucks and electrical equipment, and many older cars were upgraded. For example, 63 (formerly 11) had started life in 1902 as an open-top, unvestibuled car but was progressively modernised and is seen here in its final form in Princes Street, its motors and Brill 21E truck both being second-hand. The bulge in the vestibule accommodated the handbrake equipment. It was withdrawn on 8 September 1950 still with its wooden seats on the upper deck. *Maurice Marshall, courtesy Manchester Transport Museum Society.*

When Clarence Carter visited Stockport on 21 August 1949 he took several photographs at Mersey Square. No 53 came from a batch of ten fully-enclosed English Electric cars delivered during 1920-1921. Nicknamed 'Glasshouses', they were progressively upgraded in attempts to improve performance and reduce overall weight. Latterly they had upholstered seats, and all but one rode on 8ft-wheelbase trucks built by Cravens of Sheffield. No 53 would be the last car to receive a heavy overhaul and repaint and as such was selected to be the official 'last tram' on 25 August 1951. *C. Carter / Online Transport Archive*

After the war the Corporation wished to retain its trams, but following conversion of the last of the joint services with Manchester in January 1949, the decision was taken later the same year to scrap the town's local routes. Cravens-built No 74 is seen at Cheadle Heath in early 1951 ready to depart on the cross-town service to Reddish. Until the early 1930s trams had ventured beyond here as far as Gatley. *W. J. Wyse / LRTA (London Area)*

The operational hub was Mersey Square with its maze of tracks, loading islands and two nearby depots. Jack Wyse recorded a number of colour images in early 1951 including this broadside view of one of the English Electric cars delivered in the early 1920s. In the interests of standardisation various improvements were made to most of the cars purchased after the First World War, including the fitting of longer (8ft-wheelbase trucks), faster motors, improved gears and maroon leather seating. *W. J. Wyse / LRTA (London Area)*

LONDON

STANDARD GAUGE, CLOSED 5 JULY 1952

- London Passenger Transport Board took over nine municipal and three company tramways in 1933 with nearly 20,000 employees, 328 route miles and some 2,630 cars
- Many operators including the London County Council (LCC) tramways had invested heavily in new cars and infrastructure as had many of the operators with whom it had running agreements
- Trolleybus conversion programme interrupted by the Second World War
- 100 route miles and approximately 870 trams in 1945, all passing to the London Transport Executive in 1948
- Post-war bus shortages led to many trams being overhauled and repainted, bodies strengthened, frequencies increased, worn rail replaced and new track installed in connection with the 1951 Festival of Britain
- 'Operation Tramaway' saw a phased replacement of the system by buses between October 1950 and July 1952

On 17 May 1952, E/3 1917 is seen at The Horns, Kennington with badly war-damaged buildings on the right. *C. Carter*

What was it about London trams? They were so large, gentle, stately (yet quite fast), and they did such fascinating things which mere buses and trains did not! The shunting, reversing the seats at termini, and, above all, the conduit slot. What pleasure could be derived from watching trams slide so quickly and easily from overhead wire to conduit operation! And their exquisite motion! Three ways of swaying, sometimes all at once — side to side, front to back and that very odd business, confined to trams and dogs, of 'tail-wagging'. They did all this while making magical noises no other vehicle could, the humming and singing of the motors and the driver sounding warning by stamping on his gong pedal. Oh to hear again a hilly-route tram howling as it comes down Dog Kennel Hill, applying its magnetic brakes, or the gentle, ghostly clanking in the sepulchral darkness of the Kingsway Subway, where at stops we had to leave the car by the driver's front platform. No bus conductor ever pulled up trapdoors in the floor to fiddle about with unknown mysteries below. Yet these gentle, intriguing beasts got us home even when fog or snow stopped the buses running.

Barry Cross

Conduit operation

The conduit method of current collection was forced onto the LCC following objections to 'unsightly overhead wires'. Although a constant source of fascination for the enthusiast, it was expensive to lay and maintain and was prone to breakdowns, resulting in service disruption. How did it work? Attached to the underside of each tram was a 'plough' which passed through a continuous inch-wide channel or 'conduit', its shoes making contact with the positive and negative conductor rails. After the Second World War 90% of the system was on the conduit, and there were ten change-pits where cars switched to and from the more conventional overhead wire form of current collection. Only route 34 encountered two change-pits during its eight-mile journey, one of these being located in the middle of Gresham Road, Brixton. In this view the trolley on ex-Leyton 'E/3' No 194 has just been raised. *W. E. Robertson*

This close-up of the Gresham Road change-pit shows the protective bollards, red warning flags, lamp and Y-shaped slot layout with a line of ploughs (right), one of which is already attached to a plough fork. For the switch from conduit to overhead the tram drew to a halt, the trolley was raised, the motorman changed from conduit to overhead power via a switch on his controller and the tram moved off, shedding the plough without stopping. In reverse, while the tram moved a short distance with the pole still up, the plough was inserted into the carrier by plough shifters armed with a plough fork, the changeover controller switch was activated and the pole came down. Today it is difficult to imagine such activity in the middle of a main road. *W. E. Robertson*

Changeovers were usually completed in seconds, and between cars the plough shifters retreated to basic shelters provided after the war, by which time the elderly conduit required some 800 men to keep it going. *Dewi Williams*

Kingsway Subway

Above No other system in the UK had a subway, and no other city in the world had a conduit-operated tram tunnel for double-deckers. The journey through the half-mile subway made such an impression it even 'starred' in the legendary *Goon Show*. Influenced by early tram subways in the USA, it was operated from 1906 until 1930 by steel-bodied single-deckers and thereafter, having been completely rebuilt, by new metal-bodied double-deckers, 100 of these 'E/3'-class cars being required for its reopening in January 1931. The subway also provided a link between the north and south parts of the LCC network. As trolleybuses took over in the north, scores of redundant cars travelled via the subway to depots south of the river. The first subway route to be abandoned was the 31 in October 1950. This was followed in April 1952 by the 33 and 35. Shortly before the end an ex-LCC 'E/3' (right) waits to swing into Theobalds Road, Bloomsbury, whilst an ex-Leyton Council 'E/3' prepares to descend the ramp. The driver would have received the 'all-clear' from the signal attached to the stanchion (left). Both cars carry an illuminated 'via Kingsway Subway' sign above the destination box. *J. Law / Online Transport Archive*

Bottom Left The steps down to Aldwych Tramway Station were located in the middle of Kingsway. The obliterated place-names were those served by route 31 until 1950. The two stations within the subway, Holborn and Aldwych, had island platforms where passengers boarded cars on the offside. With a view to replacing the trams an experimental trolleybus with offside doors was tried in the subway in 1939. Large crowds witnessed the end of public service through the subway in the early hours of 6 April 1952 after which cars from Holloway depot came through either for relocation or for scrap. *J. Law / Online Transport Archive*

Bottom Right No colour images of trams in the subway have come to light. This view of one of the station names was taken during an organised visit in the early 1960s. The names were positioned so they were visible to passengers on both decks. *E. J. McWatt / Online Transport Archive*

Dog Kennel Hill
This was the only example of a four-track layout on a steeply-graded hill in the UK. Initially there had been just two tracks, but following a runaway the Board of Trade ruled that two cars must not be on the 1-in-11 gradient at the same time. As a result additional up and down tracks where added in 1912. Now four cars could be on the hill together. In October 1949 American enthusiast Bill Robertson set out to capture this spectacle in colour. After two frustrating hours he put away his camera, boarded an 84 car and, on looking back, witnessed the elusive four-tram scenario! However, during his sojourn he succeeded in taking this view with three cars. Until replaced by buses in October 1951, these 'hilly' routes were latterly the preserve of the powerful four-motor 'HR/2' cars. *W. E. Robertson*

The cars

Above left In the early years the LCC was to the fore in the design and equipping of its vehicles, notably in the introduction of fully-enclosed top decks and magnetic track brakes which allowed for faster running. Built variously by the LCC as well as by Brush and Hurst Nelson, the wooden-bodied 'E/1s' had McGuire-pattern maximum-traction bogies and were all eventually equipped for dual conduit and trolley operation. In its Munich Lake and primrose livery an 'E/1' turns from Tower Bridge Road into Tooley Street in 1926. As part of an extensive 'Pullmanisation' programme all but 200 of the entire LCC fleet were given brighter interiors, improved lighting and upholstered transverse, swing-over seats during the period 1926-30. *'The Open-Road' (1926), Claude Freise-Greene.*

Above right To the casual observer most of the 'big red trams' running after 1945 appeared alike, and in some respects they were, for the LCC had insisted that municipalities with running powers over its tracks should operate cars similar to its own standard 'E/1' design, of which more than a thousand were delivered between 1907 and 1922 making this the largest single class in England. More than half were still active in 1945, among them No 1406 which is seen shortly before it was withdrawn at New Cross Gate on 7 April 1951. It is one of a large number of E/1s built by Hurst Nelson during 1909-10; originally open-fronted the driver's windscreens were fitted in 1938. The 66 tended to be operated by the oldest cars in the fleet. *C. Carter*

Below Following the LT takeover a further mass rehabilitation programme was planned, but in the event only about 150 'E/1s' emerged from the former LCC Central Repair Works at Charlton during the period 1934-37. Classified 'E/1r', these 'rehabs' were distinguished by their flush side-panels, revised destination displays and new internal fittings. However, they retained their original trucks and electrical equipment. No 1763 of 1922 is seen close to Lambeth Palace in 1949. The last examples were withdrawn in early 1952. *W. E. Robertson*

Also withdrawn in early 1952 were the last unrebuilt 'E/1s', which, like many 'rehabs', often had loose and leaking bodywork. 1565 was one of 200 Brush-built E/1s delivered between 1910-12. In this view the trolleypole has already been raised as the car waits to go through Woolwich change-pit. The driver's windscreens were added in 1938 and 1565 was withdrawn shortly after it was photographed at Woolwich Ferry on 5 August 1951. *C. Carter*

The last 'E/1s' to enter service, in 1929-30, were Nos 552-601, which had new English Electric 'Pullman' bodies but bogies, motors and controllers salvaged from redundant single-deck subway cars. Although underpowered, many of these 'recycled' subway cars, identifiable by the wide centre pillar in the lower saloon, remained in service until the end, driver's windscreens having been added in 1939. On 8 September 1951, 560 is seen at Catford Church on the 54 which was one of the most frequent routes on the post-war system. Requiring 42 cars it ran for the last time in January 1952. Sister 'Tunnel car' 599 featured in the film *Pool of London*. C. Carter

Over the years several 'E/1s' underwent radical alterations. Following an accident 1370 was transformed into domed-roof style No 2. Emerging from Charlton in 1935, it had upholstered seats on both decks. The only 'oddity' to survive to the end, it is pictured here amongst a line of cars on Queens Road close to the major junction at New Cross Gate through which 150 cars an hour had passed through at peak times. *C. Carter*

The 'E/1' lookalikes inherited from Croydon, East Ham, West Ham and Walthamstow Corporations had a variety of different features. Crossing Westminster Bridge is one of the 25 ex-Croydon 'E/1s' (375-399) delivered during 1927-28, all having Hurst Nelson-built bodies and maximum-traction trucks, four becoming 'rehabs' in 1936. Croydon Corporation cars first reached the Embankment as late as 1926, when a connection was established with the LCC network.
W. E. Robertson collection

Mounted on standard LCC Type 4 maximum-traction trucks, Brush-bodied ex-East Ham cars 81-100 of 1927-28 were distinguished by a small route-number box in the upper-deck front window. Driver's windscreens were first fitted in 1939. After migrating south of the river the ex-East Ham cars were based at Abbey Wood depot. In this delightful study No 92 loads on the busy single-track layout in Woolwich on 5 July 1952. The 42 and 44 were the only post-war routes not to operate on the conduit. On the final day most cars carried suitable epithets. 'You'll miss me when its foggy' would prove all too true; sometimes only the trams had kept moving during frequent 'pea-soupers'.
F. E. J. Ward / Online Transport Archive

The bodies on the ex-West Ham 'E/1s' (295-312, 325-344) were built variously by the Corporation, Brush and Hurst Nelson between 1925 and 1931 and were distinguishable by the small, squat number boxes beneath the front upper-deck windows as well as the narrow moulding surrounding the side advertising space. Although more sluggish than their sprightly East Ham neighbours many survived to the end. Unlike other operators LT retained the wartime masks fitted to the headlights, claiming they provided a stronger rear light. Although trams served Victoria and came within striking distance of Big Ben and the Houses of Parliament they never penetrated the capital's major commercial and financial districts. This was due to early opposition to unsightly overhead wires and fears that the lower orders might 'invade' the more prosperous areas of the capital. Many south London routes ran along Victoria Embankment, cars displaying different numbers when working clockwise or anti-clockwise. For example, on 30 June 1952 ex-West Ham 342 was on an anti-clockwise 36 to Abbey Wood; when working clockwise to the same terminus cars showed '38'.
J. B. C. McCann / Online Transport Archive

Nicknamed 'Rockets', the Walthamstow 'E/1s' were noisy and rough-riding but they were also fast and were capable of maintaining the same speeds as the Felthams. Built in two batches, 2042-2053 (Hurst Nelson, 1927) and 2054-2061 (Brush, 1932), the last examples survived in passenger service until January 1952. On 5 August 1951, 2053 has just passed through Woolwich change-pit ready to make the long run to The Embankment. *C. Carter*

New trams delivered to the LCC during the early 1930s still bore a strong resemblance to the 'Pullmanised' 'E/1s'. Included were two batches of powerful cars classified 'HR/2', the letters denoting their suitability for hilly routes. Nos 1854-1903 of 1930 had flush-sided English Electric bodies, four motors, hand and magnetic brakes, special electric 'run-back' brakes for use on steep hills, EMB equal-wheel bogies (except for 1898, which was fitted with EMB radial-arm axleboxes) and plough-carriers mounted on the body underframes. Windscreens were added between 1936 and 1939. 1879 is seen at Catford Bridge on route 58 on the 8 September 1951, just weeks before the closure of the Dulwich area routes. After this most of the HR/2s saw several more months service although 1879 was withdrawn before the final closure. *C. Carter*

Nos 101-160 of 1931 were the first totally enclosed cars delivered to the LCC and were unique in having no trolley poles. This restricted these Hurst Nelson cars to conduit-only routes such as the 58 Victoria-Blackwall Tunnel. In this view 105 passes through Rushey Green on 8 September 1951. Equipped with equal-wheel bogies incorporating EMB radial-arm axleboxes and helical gears, the 'trolleyless' 'HR/2s' lasted until replacement of the last all-conduit route, the 14-mile 35 from Highgate to Forest Hill, in April 1952. Historically, when the bogies under 160 passed to LCC No 1 it received maximum traction bogies making it the only 'trolleyless' 'E/3'. *C. Carter*

Designed for the remodelled Kingsway Subway, the 100 'E/3s' (1904-2003) of 1931 had all-metal, flush-sided bodies by Hurst Nelson and rode on EMB maximum-traction bogies. No 1939 is seen outside New Cross depot on 5 July 1952. With accommodation for 314 trams on 32 tracks, this was the largest of the LCC depots. Latterly it had a reputation for mediocre maintenance and poor labour relations, and lines of cars often piled up outside, awaiting crew changes. London was the last system in the British Isles to use route stencil plates, which were back-lit at night. *F. E. J. Ward / Online Transport Archive*

When the LCC took over operation of the Leyton Council tramways in 1921 the latter continued to provide rolling stock. In 1931 50 'E/3'-type cars (161-210) were delivered with English Electric bodies. In this view 179 passes a replacement bus as it works clockwise along the Embankment on the 38 ready for the long journey to Abbey Wood. Right to the end the combined 36/38 routes required just under 60 cars. *C. Carter*

Above left Named after the location of the Union Construction Co, which built the bodywork, the 100 'Felthams' were the most distinctive trams to pass to LT. Placed in service during 1930-31, they owed their revolutionary design to earlier experiments. When transferred to LT, the 54 Metropolitan Electric Tramways (MET) 'Felthams' became 2066-2119 and the 46 from the London United 2120-2165. One of the former, 2088 is seen outside Telford Avenue depot in 1948. Way ahead of their time, these imposing 64-seat cars had all-metal bodies, straight staircases, no internal bulkheads and large vestibules for some 20 standees (later reduced following Trade Union pressure), passenger flow with a front exit (later disused), EMB maximum-traction bogies, air brakes, body-mounted plough-carriers and a separate, projecting driver's cab. 90 of these cars were sold for further service in Leeds. *J. Law / Online Transport Archive*

Above right The experimental 'Bluebird' of 1932 was intended as the forerunner of a proposed fleet of 100 luxury cars for use on the Kingsway Subway routes. Built by the LCC and initially painted in Royal blue and ivory-cream, No 1 had an all-metal domed-roof body, comfortable seats, linoleum floor-covering, EMB equal-wheel heavyweight bogies, air brakes, air-operated jack-knife doors, saloon heaters, separate driver's cabs, windscreen wipers and a body-mounted plough-carrier. Sadly it remained a one-off. After being painted in traditional red and transferred to Telford Avenue depot in the late 1930s it had a chequered career as a rush-hour extra, its last spell in service being from 1946 until 1951. However, like the 'Felthams' it did influence the design of vehicles built for other undertakings. As part of enthusiast tour to mark the demise of the Croydon routes it ventured through the subway as far as Archway on 7 April 1951. After withdrawal it saw further service in Leeds until 1957. *Tom Marsh / Online Transport Archive*

Left The passing of the London trams during the night of 5/6 July 1952 marked the end of conduit operation in Britain. This excellent view was taken at Woolwich. To avoid congestion in the vicinity of the change-pit seen in the background, eastbound cars often formed a queue waiting their turn to go through. To avoid blocking the busy road down to the Woolwich Free Ferry (left) the queue began some distance from the change-pit which often allowed time for the trolley to be raised in advance (as on ex-West Ham 342) so that the car could go through the pit and shoot its plough without stopping. Trolleybuses were also able to pass the waiting trams on the nearside. In the opposite direction, there was only the pair of trolleybus wires. Most change pits had cross-overs on either side so cars could be turned in case of problems. Just about to leave the change-pit at 3.30pm on 8 September 1951 is an ex-Croydon car. *C. Carter*

Although the conduit often caused problems and delays, latterly the overhead also suffered from a degree of neglect with the result that emergency repairs and checks had to be carried out. Here a tower wagon is in attendance at Middle Park Avenue on 17 May 1952. 'Tunnel car' 560 and E/3 1909 are both on the 46. This area witnessed some of the last LCC tramway extensions in the early 1930s. *C. Carter*

BIRMINGHAM

3FT 6IN GAUGE, CLOSED 4 JULY 1953

- Largest 3ft 6in-gauge system in the UK
- Maximum route mileage: 79
- Maximum number of cars in service: 825
- First electric line in the city – 1901
- First Corporation electric line – 1904
- Many terminal loops in the central area — no cross-city routes
- Reserved-track sections opened 1919-38
- Bow collectors used on specific routes
- Abandonment 1922-53

Once dubbed 'the city of a thousand trades', Birmingham manufactured tramcars from 1862 until the 1960s for Britain and for many other countries. It operated horse, steam, cable, battery and overhead-line electric trams (as such being unique in the UK), but it excluded them at an early stage from major central streets and squares and from cross-city services. It was obliged to adopt a narrow gauge because of the local topography; as a consequence it was not allowed to enclose the upper-deck balconies of the four-wheel cars, and both they and the bogie double-deckers presented a slim, so-called 'consumptive' look when viewed end-on. But they could be speedy, sometimes inducing fears on the part of uninitiated faint-hearted passengers that their vehicle might topple over. And, to the whine of the magnetic track brake, they could stop on the proverbial sixpence. Maintained in superb condition, they remained immaculate in their dark-blue and cream livery to the end.

G. B. Claydon

Reserved tracks
Between 1919 and 1938 certain sections of street track were relocated onto reservations, usually in the centre of dual carriageways. In addition, many miles of new reserved track were laid between 1920 and 1928, mostly to serve new suburban housing estates developed under the Corporation's policy of re-housing people away from the overcrowded central area. Car 534 is seen on Pebble Mill Road reservation just months before this section was abandoned in July 1952. Latterly, cars 512-536 had 70hp motors. *C. Carter*

The fleet

The Corporation's first tram route opened in January 1904 and was operated by open-top bogie cars Nos 1-20 built by the United Electric Car Co, of which six survived (in much-altered form) until 1949. Top covers were fitted shortly after delivery; then, during the 1920s, they were rebuilt with four-window saloons, driver's vestibules, normal half-turn stairs and transverse seats on the lower deck. They were also re-trucked and given more powerful motors. Only six survived the war, one of which, 17, is seen at Dale End on 9 July 1949. It has EMB bogies and two 40hp motors. At a height of 16ft 6in these cars were unable to pass under low bridges so spent virtually all their lives on route 6 (Perry Barr), which closed with effect from 1 January 1950. *C. Carter / Online Transport Archive*

Early on the Board of Trade had stipulated that no narrow-gauge four-wheel car could have a fully-enclosed upper deck. As a result Birmingham became the last system to operate narrow-gauge open-balcony cars in all-day service. Between 1905 and 1913 a total of 430 had entered service, these comprising a mix of three- and four-window UEC-built cars on a variety of trucks, the majority being delivered with open-canopy top covers. Over the years they acquired driver's vestibules, better seating, different trucks and new motors and controllers. During his visit to Birmingham on 9 July 1949 Clarence Carter took several rare colour photographs, including this shot of 420 loading on Digbeth for the run out to Alcester Lanes End. This was one of 50 four-window cars delivered during 1912-13 with 7ft 6in Mountain & Gibson radial trucks and special Spencer oil and air track brakes which allowed the cars to operate on the steep 1-in-13 grade in Leopold Street. The original longitudinal seating in the lower saloon was replaced in the 1920s by more comfortable 2+1 transverse seating. Similar cars from the '301' class remained as rush-hour extras until September 1950, and one of these, 395, is now preserved. The car is in the dark-blue and primrose livery with shaded numerals. *C. Carter / Online Transport Archive*

Above Between 1913 and 1930 a total of 331 maximum traction bogie cars (512-843) entered service, with a variety of different bodies, trucks, motors, controllers and brakes, and of these some 262 were still active in 1951. Some of the oldest survived to the end, and one of these is seen at Pype Hayes Park in July 1953. Built by UEC in 1913-14 as open-balcony cars, 512-586 were delivered with 'Burnley'-type maximum-traction bogies. During the 1920s most were refitted with upholstered transverse seating on both decks, and all were top-covered during the period 1926-31, 581 retaining the original four-window arrangement. In 1943 it was fitted with EMB 'Burnley' bogies and 40hp motors from war-damaged cars. It is in the later simplified, unlined livery with plain numerals. *W. S. Eades / Online Transport Archive*

Opposite This view at Erdington terminus clearly shows the 'Burnley' style of maximum-traction bogies devised by Henry Mozley, Manager of the 4ft gauge Burnley system. By repositioning the side bearing springs Mozley enabled the large driving wheels at the front to take up to 80% of the overall weight of the car, thereby partially alleviating the stresses and strains of braking and acceleration. The guiding axle was also held down by a coil spring in compression, which helped to stop derailments. 'Burnley' bogies, obtained from different manufacturers, were used under 512-843. Most of these cars latterly weighed nearly 17 tons and had seating varying from 60 to 63. *W.S. Eades / Online Transport Archive*

Brush-built cars 587-636 of 1920-21 were the last to be delivered with open balconies. These were subsequently enclosed between 1927 and 1931. Later, over 50 of the class were fitted with improved motors. Most had upholstered transverse seats fitted to both decks during the 1920s. Subsequently some underwent further alterations. One of the class is seen on the right of this view taken at Gravelly Hill junction which is now totally subsumed under today's 'Spaghetti Junction'. From here outbound cars on the last three routes — 2, 78 and 79 — headed in different directions whilst city-bound cars were marshalled into the correct order for reversing at the city terminus in Steelhouse Lane. *W. J. Wyse / LRTA (London Area)*

All cars after 636 were fully enclosed, and the first batch to enter service, in 1923 (637-661) had Midland Railway Carriage & Wagon Company bodies and 42 hp motors. Within a few years the original wooden seating had, in most cases, been replaced on both decks by transverse, upholstered seating. Most survived into 1953, and 640 is seen passing the Central Fire Station (left) as it heads out of the city along Aston Street towards Pype Hayes Park on 24 May 1952. *C. Carter*

Above The last all-electric cars to be delivered came in three batches between 1924 and 1926. 662-731 had Brush bodies and were powered by a mix of 40hp and 42hp motors. Towards the end of its life, 700 of 1925 is pictured at Short Heath terminus. Many of this class were destroyed or badly damaged during air-raids on two depots. This car carries the simplified post-war version of the cobalt and primrose livery first introduced in 1946. *W. S. Eades / Online Transport Archive*

With its dearth of cross-city services, trams in Birmingham terminated on a series of loops and stubs in or near the heart of the city, most being within easy reach of the administrative, commercial and entertainment districts as well as the principal railway stations. The last of the city termini to be served by trams was Steelhouse Lane where all-electric car 729 is seen on 24 May 1952 prior to its run to Erdington. It required considerable organisation to keep the non-stop procession of cars reversing here in the correct order. Reflecting the intense level of service, there were still over 100 cars available for the three remaining routes in June 1953. *C. Carter*

Left In 1926 Birmingham took delivery of another batch of Brush-built 60-seaters, Nos 732-761. These 'fast' cars were powered by two 63hp English Electric motors, and all had air track brakes. They were the first trams to have upholstered transverse seats on the upper deck. Long associated with the Bristol Road routes they were all withdrawn when these services were replaced in July 1952. Car 752 is seen at Navigation Street terminus on 24 May 1952 waiting to depart for Rednal shortly before the routes were abandoned. On bank holidays, scores of extra trams had been drafted onto the Rednal service which provided access to the Lickey Hills. The plated over bulkhead on the car behind 752 indicates that its body had been strengthened. The imposing building in the background is the Birmingham Municipal Technical College of 1895. *C. Carter*

Below Delivered during 1928-29, Brush-built cars 762-811 were equipped with bow collectors and allocated to Washwood Heath depot for use on routes 8 and 10. Distinguished by their eight independently-operated windows on the upper deck, they had 63hp motors and EMB air wheel and track brakes. Complete with pram on the platform, 803 is at Dale End on 9 July 1949. Most of this area of the city would later be redeveloped. Following closure of routes 8 and 10 in 1950 most of the bow-collector cars were equipped with trolley poles and worked the Bristol Road routes until July 1952. The eight window style of top deck was developed as an attempt to give individual passengers more control over the ventilation. Very often, upper decks could be lost in a fug of tobacco smoke. *C. Carter / Online Transport Archive*

Built by Short Bros and delivered in 1929, 812-841 were long associated with the Pershore Road routes. They had seats for 60, eight windows upstairs and English Electric 63hp motors. Their 'Burnley' bogies, air wheel and track, brakes were supplied by Maley & Taunton. On these cars, each brake could be operated separately by the motorman. On 24 May 1952, 818 is outbound to Cotteridge on Pebble Mill Road. This view was taken during the conversion of Selly Oak depot when lines of cars were parked on the city bound track between September 1951 and July 1952. New crossovers were installed and movements along the single line were controlled by coloured light signals, one of which can be seen on the traction pole. *C. Carter*

56

Above Seen on route 36 on 9 July 1949, 828 was another of the 1929 cars all but one of which survived until July 1952. Birmingham was unusual in that the indicator displays on the cars mostly remained the same throughout the day. Only the route number was shown at either end of the car with the route detail appearing in the side indicator boxes only. The green Bundy clocks were used to regulate time-keeping across the network. *C. Carter / Online Transport Archive*

Below In 1929 and 1930 the Corporation took delivery of 842 and 843, two experimental, all-metal lightweight cars. Built by Brush, 843 (seen here) was the city's last new tram and had seats for 60, Maley & Taunton maximum-traction bogies, 40hp motors and air, wheel and track brakes. Both cars were assigned to Cotteridge depot. 843 was withdrawn in January 1952 and 842 in the July with both being broken up the following month. *B. C. Sexton / National Tramway Museum*

BELFAST

4FT 9IN GAUGE, CLOSED 28 FEBRUARY 1954

- All street track
- Last extension 1925, last new trams 1935
- Abandonment 1938-1954
- Late use of balcony cars
- Some cars with unusual upper-deck window arrangement
- Rare instance of trams' terminating inside railway stations
- Queen's Road route on land owned by the Belfast Harbour Commissioners
- At the end trams operated during peak hours only

I first visited Belfast with Roy Brook and was thrilled to find some tramcars similar to Cardiff's. Travelling along Queen's Road, to the left were the yards of Harland & Woolf, whilst the right was flanked by warehouses. To my surprise a track led straight into the BCDR station concourse at a right angle to the trains. The next surprise occurred at 3.30pm. Tramcars started to appear, not one or two but many. By 4.30pm there were about 35-40 cars parked awaiting the homeward rush. Next day we visited Mt Pottinger depot, home of the peak hour fleet. To witness the speed with which cars left the depot, made two reversals on disused track at Castlereagh Junction and made off for Queen's Quay was an unforgettable sight which I still recall fondly some 60 years later.

R. W. A. Jones

Visitors to Belfast were fascinated by the sheer volume of traffic along Queen's Road and long rush hour queues in the vicinity of Queen's Bridge. Even after the all-day tram service ceased a dwindling number of peak hour cars continued transporting thousands of shipyard workers until February 1954.
W. E. Robertson / Colour-Rail IR414

The fleet
The 170 trams delivered for the opening were typical three-window, open top cars with Brush-built bodies, Brill 21E trucks and two 25hp motors. Known as 'Standard Reds' (after the former horse-car livery), they were all fitted with top covers after 1907. Unusually the covered area on the upper deck was quite short, as can be seen in this rare pre-war line-up taken during Coronation Week 1937. The car in front is displaying a wooden 'via' board in the offside front window.
Reg Ludgate collection / Colour-Rail IR474

Similar to the 'Standard Reds', some 60 cars were built by the Corporation between 1908 and 1913, their upper decks being to an unusual design. Along with a number of 'Standard Reds' some were rebuilt between 1929 and 1932 as fully-enclosed cars with upholstered transverse seats and more powerful motors. Amongst the 'rebuilds' were 251 and 164. The latter, the first of the 50 to be rebuilt, was also the first to be painted in a striking new livery of princess blue and white. The deep centre windows in the middle of the upper deck were probably unique to Belfast. Some of these sturdy cars survived until 1953 and were often employed as 'shipyard specials' serving Harland & Woolf. *W. E. Robertson*

Belfast named groups of cars after particular general managers. Ordered by James Moffett and delivered during the early 1920s, 292-341 had 68-seat Brush bodies, Peckham pendulum P22 trucks, 40hp motors and number and destination indicators in the upper-deck front windows. Originally painted red and cream, the 'Moffetts' appeared in Princess Blue after the majority were rebuilt in the early 1930s with upholstered seats, more powerful motors and air brakes. At the same time, the small front-exit door located behind the stairs on the offside was removed. Here the crew of 295 take their layover at Queen's Quay in June 1952. *Ian Davidson / Colour-Rail IR523*

Nos 342-391 of 1930 were built to the specification of General Manager William Chamberlain, who had come from Leeds. They had Brush bodies (some being assembled by a local firm, Service Motor Works), upholstered transverse seating for 68, Maley & Taunton 8ft-wheelbase swing-link trucks, two 50hp motors and air wheel and air track brakes. After taking shipyard workers along Queen's Road, Brush-bodied 374 is *en route* to Mt Pottinger depot in October 1953. In the final months only 'Chamberlains' remained, 12 forming the final procession on 28 February 1954. *W. E. Robertson*

Opposite top Dating from 1935, 392-441 were designed by and named after General Manager Robert McCreary. They had the same trucks and equipment as the 'Chamberlains', with bodies by English Electric, of which the larger proportion were assembled by Service Motor Works, each group having minor design and livery differences. When American enthusiast Bill Robertson discovered the Ligoneil routes were to close, he flew from the US in October 1953. Among his views is this splendid scene of a 'McCreary' processing along Royal Avenue. The bodies, with their domed roofs, curved ends and platform doors, proved less robust than those on the 'Chamberlains', and the 64 seat 'McCrearys' were withdrawn en masse with effect from 11 October 1953. To staff and public they were always the 'Streamliners'. The traction poles had been painted silver for the Coronation of HM Queen Elizabeth II. Most of these buildings still survive, although the thoroughfare is now pedestrian-only. *W. E. Robertson*

Opposite bottom left Northern Ireland once relied almost entirely on coal from the mainland. In this view of Queen's Quay cranes are busy off-loading coal into the various merchants' yards and a Fordson lorry, with domestic supplies, is parked on the east side of Station Street. Visible beyond 'Chamberlain' 351 are the tracks leading to/from Queen's Quay railway station. *W. E. Robertson*

Opposite bottom right The city was unusual in having two railway stations with internal tram sidings, the single-car bay at Queen's Quay surviving until 1953. For many years trams met most principal trains, and this undercover interchange proved very useful during inclement weather. The entire station was subsequently demolished. The original directional arrows on this 'McCreary' have been plated over. *W. E. Robertson*

SUNDERLAND

STANDARD GAUGE, CLOSED 1 OCTOBER 1954

- Greatest variety of cars on any post-war UK system
- Major rebuilding programmes undertaken by managers Dayson (1903-29) and Hopkins (1929-48) plus investment in new cars
- Extensive purchases of quality second hand trams
- Bow collectors from 1929, subsequently replaced by pantographs, 1933-49.
- First route closure 1928
- 94 trams in 1948
- Every tram advertised 'Shop at Binns'
- 13¾ route miles
- One of the last first-generation tramway extensions.

In 1951, at the age of 14, I cycled from Newcastle upon Tyne to Sunderland to ride on the trams, parking my unlocked bicycle on spare ground. Use of the pantograph fascinated me, as did a few 'straight crossovers' with 'made-up' main line — a bumpy ride for reversing cars. Charles Hopkins' second-hand purchases from seven systems gave a wonderful variety of trams. Routes too varied widely, the Circle Line's terraced streets in Millfield and Roker contrasting with the impressive Victorian seafront villas leading to Roker and Seaburn, the single-track football-ground loop, the terminus actually on the pavement at Grangetown. The Durham Road route took you through more terraced houses, past 1930s 'semis' and into a post-war housing estate with more than a mile of reserved track. And the bike? It was still there!

Hugh McAulay

Durham Road extension, 1948-49
Sunderland was noted for a short-lived post-war ¾ mile extension which was opened shortly after the decision had been taken to scrap the trams. Built to serve new housing estates along Durham Road, it was on a central reservation in the middle of a dual carriageway; however owing to the gradients, only air brake cars were normally used. In this panoramic view an ex-Ilford car approaches the terminus. The last section, opened in February 1949, did not incorporate ballast laid to the rail-head but left the sleepers and tie-bars exposed so that the track could be easily removed when the line closed in 1954. The *Prospect Hotel* can be seen on the right. *J. Copland, courtesy Martin Jenkins / Online Transport Archive*

Veteran rebuilds

Sea Lane was a favourite location for photographers. By the early 1950s the oldest trams were much-rebuilt survivors from the original fleet of 65 cars built by the Electric Railway & Tramway Carriage Works. No15 was from a batch of six open-top six-window bogie cars dating from 1900. Although their bogies were replaced by four-wheel trucks as early as 1901 they were always known as the 'Bogie' cars to the end! No15 was the last of the group to be rebuilt in the early 1930s, when it was given extended platforms, transverse seats in the lower saloon, normal stairs, a fourth truck (a Peckham P22) and reconditioned 40hp motors. The 58-seat car was withdrawn in March 1953. *R. W. A. Jones / Online Transport Archive*

Sunderland certainly knew how to maximise the life of their trams. No 22 had started life in 1901 as one of eight four-wheel single-deckers. In 1925, 22 was one of three of the cars to be rebuilt by the Corporation as a fully-enclosed 68-seat double-decker. Then in the early 1930s it was given an 8ft 6in-wheelbase truck, two 45hp motors and air brakes. It was withdrawn early in 1954. *B. C. Sexton / National Tramway Museum*

Entering service in 1902 as one of 10 open-top four-wheelers, 63 was rebuilt in 1933 as a fully-enclosed car with new staircases, lengthened platforms, an English Electric truck and two 62hp motors. Note the mismatched three-window lower deck and four-window upper deck — a not uncommon feature when the two decks of an upgraded tram were often decades apart. It was withdrawn in January 1954. *B. C. Sexton / National Tramway Museum*

Above One of the most remarkable rebuilds was No 84. Emerging from Hylton Road works in 1926, this totally-enclosed double-decker incorporated parts from a former Sunderland & District Electric Tramways Brush-built car of 1908 which had ended its days on the interurban system (which once connected with Sunderland) as a parcels car. In 1931, it was given an 8ft 6in EMB swing link truck and improved brakes, motors and controllers. It is seen here at Seaburn at 12.30pm on 24 August 1952 signed as a shorting working to Fawcett Street. It was withdrawn in March 1953. *C. Carter*

Left Seen here at Dykelands Road in 1951, 68 was one of six Brush-built balcony cars (66-71) delivered in 1906. When Archibald Dayson was Manager these 66-seaters were rebuilt as fully enclosed with new stairs and dashes; then, under Manager Charles Hopkins, they received lengthened platforms and transverse upholstered seats in the lower saloon. At the same time 68 was given an English Electric truck and two 42hp motors. It was withdrawn in June 1953.
W. J. Wyse / LRTA (London Area)

Front exit

Following trends on Tyneside, Sunderland's first fully-enclosed cars (72-83) had English Electric front-exit 58-seat bodies when delivered during 1921-22. When the arrangement proved unsuccessful the front exits were removed and the platforms lengthened when the cars were rebuilt between 1929 and 1932. In this view 76 is crossing the Wearmouth Bridge in the early 1950s by which time it had an EMB truck and two 50hp motors. It remained in service until December 1952. *W.J.Wyse / LRTA(London Area)*

The modern fleet

Owing to its silent running and the secrecy surrounding its construction at the Corporation's workshops at Hylton Road No 86 of 1932 was dubbed 'the Ghost Tram'. This well-appointed vehicle had comfortable seats for 62, flush sides, a new streamline livery and air brakes. It was followed in 1933 by 12 similar cars — 87-95 built by English Electric and 96-98 by the Corporation. Known as the 'Durham Road' cars they had 9ft-wheelbase EMB roller-bearing trucks and two 62hp motors. In 1954 No 98, the first Sunderland car to be equipped with a pantograph, is involved in a crew change outside Wheat Sheaf depot and Head Office. In the background is the *Wheatsheaf* Hotel and the lighthouse which formed part of the premises of Will's the Grocers. Also on view are a Triumph Dolomite and a utility Guy in the Corporation's green and white bus livery. *J. Copland*

Built at Hylton Road in 1935, 26-28 were modified versions of the 'Durham Road' cars with similar equipment. These 64-seaters featured twin headlights, domed roofs with eaves glasses and luxury contemporary interiors yet reintroduced quarterlight ventilators in the lower saloon — a feature redolent of earlier decades. The ubiquitous 'Shop at Binns' adverts on Sunderland trams were first introduced in 1921. All were withdrawn during 1953. *B. C. Sexton / National Tramway Museum*

In 1934, Sunderland purchased a luxury centre-entrance bogie car from English Electric. Although the car proved expensive to operate, it was decided some of its features should be incorporated into a less-expensive four wheel version. As a result two 60-seat, centre-entrance cars, one built by the Corporation (54) and one by Brush (55) entered service during 1935-36. Centre entrances in four-wheeled cars meant that there was no space for a dropped underframe so the side frames of their 9ft wheelbase Maley & Taunton trucks had to be profiled to accommodate the platform and steps. No 55 is seen on 17 May 1949 in the red and cream livery first introduced in 1935 in which the coat of arms was encased in a cream diamond and the fleet number in a red square. 55 was withdrawn in June 1953. *C. Carter / Online Transport Archive*

The bodies on 49-52, which entered service between 1938 and 1940, were built at Hylton Road on frames supplied by English Electric, the design having more than an echo of Blackpool's 'Balloon' double-deckers. As with 54 and 55, the truck side frames (this time by English Electric) were specially contoured to accommodate the entrance well. Although fine cars they never seemed to recover from wartime neglect and appeared battered and unloved by the end of their days. Only two remained when the Circle route closed in January 1954.
R. W. A Jones / Online Transport Archive

Second-hand cars

Between 1931 and 1948 Sunderland acquired some 30 second-hand trams, including the body shells of two English Electric cars built for Mansfield & District in 1925. They were used in the construction of 21 and 24 at Hylton Road. Entering service in 1933, they had resilient-riding EMB 'hornless'-type trucks, two 62hp motors and, so they could work system-wide, air, wheel and magnetic track brakes. Retaining its wooden upper-deck seats to the end, 24 turns from Gladstone Street into Roker Street in 1954. Note the three nuns in the background. *J. Copland*

During 1937-38 a non-standard centre-entrance 'Feltham' was acquired from London Transport together with eight 60-seat four-wheelers built by Brush for Ilford Corporation in 1932. On arrival the latter were fitted with vestibules, new stairs and the height of the lower decks was reduced. At the same time their 50hp motors were rewound to produce a higher speed. Between 1946 and 1948 they were given new Maley & Taunton hornless trucks and air brakes, allowing them to work on the Durham Road route. In 1954 No 5 is on Fulwell Road at the crossing with the goods-only branch down to North Docks.
J. Copland, courtesy Martin Jenkins / Online Transport Archive

Above It is generally agreed that the eight cars acquired from Huddersfield in 1938 were the best of Manager Hopkins' second-hand purchases. Apart from re-gauging from Huddersfield's non-standard 4ft 7³/₄in and removal of platform doors, very little alteration was needed, and the cars were in such good condition they entered service without repainting in their home-town livery of red and cream. Built by English Electric in 1931-32, they had Maley & Taunton swing-axle trucks of 8ft 6in wheelbase, two 50hp motors and air wheel and track brakes, enabling them to operate system-wide. No 33 is seen in North Bridge Street in 1953. Most lasted until the end. *D. A. Jones*

Opposite bottom The last one-off was purchased in 1948. Formerly Bury Corporation 30, it dated from 1905 but had been much rebuilt. Latterly it had an EMB truck of 8ft 6in wheelbase, two 50hp motors, air brakes and seats for 58. One enthusiast remembers it well. 'That little car that went to Sunderland was a favourite of mine. It had a much more modern truck than any other at Bury, and although it looked unremarkable — even dowdy — it had a turn of speed that was probably the reason Sunderland snapped it up.' It must have been considered a worthy acquisition, for 85 lasted until March 1954. It was among several cars not to have the diamond surround to the coat of arms. *B. C. Sexton / National Tramway Museum*

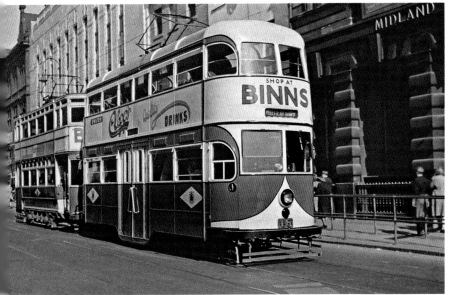

Top left It was inconceivable that Hopkins with his finger on the pulse of tramway closures, would not take part in the 'lucky dip' sales of Manchester's 38 Pullman ('Pilcher') cars, which became available from 1946 onwards. The six acquired by Sunderland were numbered 37-42. Built between 1930 and 1932, they were mounted on Peckham P35 trucks but, having no air-brakes, they were unsuitable for the hilly Durham Road route. The last four, including 37, were withdrawn in early 1954. Hopkins died shortly after these cars were delivered and was succeeded by HW Snowball, who continued to keep the system in good order. *B. C. Sexton / National Tramway Museum*

One-offs
Top right Hopkins believed in the advantages of a well-run modern tram system. Among his acquisitions were several quality 'one-offs' acquired at bargain prices. A case in point was Sunderland No 45. It first entered service in Portsmouth in 1930 and was designed by their Manager Ben Hall. On arrival at Hylton Road in 1936, the 53-seater was given new staircases and later, in 1938, an EMB swing-axle truck of 8ft 6in wheelbase and two 50hp motors. It had smooth in-swept lower-deck sides, and the roof sticks were exposed within the upper deck. It was withdrawn in 1953. Here it leaves the impressive Wearmouth Bridge (1929) heading for the town centre. *W. J. Wyse / LRTA (London Area)*

Centre Another one-off came from near neighbour South Shields in 1946. Like ex-Portsmouth No 1 this English Electric built centre-entrance car had been intended as the forerunner of a new fleet. Also dating from 1936, the design featured a noticeably rounder profile, with longer windows and a single headlamp. A bargain at £250, it had a Maley & Taunton truck, air brakes and two 50hp motors. On arrival it was hardly altered except for the addition of roof-drainage external rainwater conductors (of the small-bore copper-tube variety). Given the number 48, it is pictured in Fawcett Street on 17 May 1949 waiting to depart for Villette Road, a route abandoned in November 1950. Behind is one of the two ex-Accrington Brush-built cars acquired in 1931 both of which were withdrawn in 1953. *C. Carter / Online Transport Archive*

LLANDUDNO & COLWYN BAY

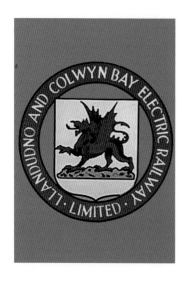

3FT 6IN GAUGE, CLOSED 25 MARCH 1956

- Last company-owned tramway in the UK
- Last narrow gauge tramway on the mainland
- Last regular use of open-toppers and totally open 'toastracks'
- Second-hand acquisitions
- Use of a private toll road
- Subject of failed preservation scheme

For me the tram ride from Llandudno to Colwyn Bay and back on a summer's day was a must. Seeing the variety of trams pass by, the home-made shelters at remote stops, single-line working along the seashore and catching a glimpse of the tram sheds, with a few cars in the yard basking in the sunshine, was all utterly enchanting. And that exhilarating experience of the fast descent, on the front seat of a toastrack, from the top of Penrhyn Hill down through Bodafon fields and across the plain towards Llandudno remains unforgettable.

Geoff Price

The route and the fleet
This delightful tramway linking the seaside resorts of Llandudno, Rhos-on-Sea and Colwyn Bay had something for everyone — superb sea and mountain vistas, original and second-hand cars, street running, single track and loops, interlaced track, reserved track including a steeply-graded hillside section as well as tracks along a private road complete with toll booths. One of the increasing number of photographers to visit the tramway during 1955 was John McCann. On 9 July motorman John Glyn Jones is at the controls as No 20 as it makes its way from Palladium Corner, Llandudno, down to West Shore. Delivered in 1920, this was one of four 60-seat English Electric-built 'toastracks' (19-22) with two 37hp motors. In the background is the imposing *Odeon* cinema (since demolished) with its ballroom and cafeteria, while alongside is the boarding point for tours operated by Cream's coaches. *J. B. C. McCann / Online Transport Archive*

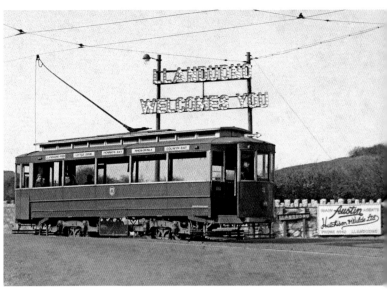

Above left In 1936 the company replaced some of its original single-deckers with ten open-toppers acquired from Bournemouth. These 66-seaters (6-15) provided much-needed additional capacity on fine days, when loadings could be exceptionally heavy and 'extras' were needed. Except for No 6 all the ex-Bournemouth cars had Brush-built bodies, Brill 22E bogies and were constructed between 1921 and 1926. On 18 September 1955, No 15 is on Mostyn Broadway. In the background are the *Grand* (1901), used by the BBC Variety Department during the Second World War, and to the left the less imposing *Arcadia* (since demolished), home to the famous 'Catlin Follies', widely advertised on the trams. Alongside was a large Crosville bus depot, now closed. The crossover in the foreground was installed in 1954 and enabled 'extras' to deal with audiences leaving the two venues. Latterly the rail on this section was badly worn and heavily corrugated. Note the ornate gas-lamp to the left of the tram. *J. B. C. McCann / Online Transport Archive*

Above right With an eye for bargains, the Company purchased five Brush-built 40-seater single-deckers from Accrington Corporation in 1932, three of which came as bodies. On arrival, these were given equal wheel bogies from withdrawn cars and one of these No 3 is seen at the top of Penrhyn Hill in 1955. The lightly-loaded car is making for Colwyn Bay with its trolley virtually at full stretch. All these single-deckers originally entered service in Accrington red and cream but were later repainted in the green and cream livery introduced in 1933. *W. G. S. Hyde / Online Transport Archive*

Below left From Craig-y-Don to Penrhyn Bay the line had interurban characteristics, including a cross-country reservation through Bodafon Fields which afforded passengers superb views of the surrounding scenery. *J. B. C. McCann / Online Transport Archive*

Below right The most spectacular section on the 7¹/₂ mile line was this reservation carved into the side of Penrhyn Hill, the steepest part of which was 1 in 11. During the descent drivers exercised due caution and made skilful use of the hand and wheel brakes whilst conductors occupied the rear platform to ensure that the trolley stayed on the wire. No 13 is close to the site of a siding which once served a stone-crushing plant. When the line was abandoned the adjacent road was widened by swallowing up this hillside section. *J. B. C. McCann / Online Transport Archive*

At Penrhyn Bay successive sea encroachments led to closure of the unstable track on the seaward side during the winter of 1952. As a result single-line working was introduced, and the overhead realigned. With work on the sea defences taking place in the background, Llandudno-bound 'rack' 19 waits for an approaching car to clear the single line. Stretching into the distance is the company-owned Marine Drive, while to the left is the toll-house, where the keeper collected monies and issued tickets to any vehicles using the road. A special anemometer was located here to gauge the strength of the wind; this ensured crews took particular care on exposed sections of the line. On the left of this view taken on 9 July 1955 are a Standard 8 and a Ford Consul. *J. B. C. McCann / Online Transport* Archive

Latterly only two of the original 14 cars remained. Built in 1907 by the Midland Railway Carriage & Wagon Company and designed for light-railway work, they had two compartments and two doors per side, single trolleys, four 30hp motors and Mountain & Gibson equal-wheel bogies. Over the years they received double trolleys, less-powerful motors and replacement controllers, and a door on each side was blocked off. Seen here at Rhos-on-Sea depot, 17 was earmarked to be the official 'last tram' but in the event was scrapped prematurely following an accident. *J. B. C. McCann / Online Transport Archive*

Relatively few early colour views exist of interiors. This portrait highlights the varnished lower-deck ceiling, panelled woodwork, saloon door, large panes of glass, strap hangers and fare sheets on ex-Bournemouth No 8. During 1953-54 many cars were re-fitted with moquette seating acquired from Birmingham Corporation. *B. C. Sexton / National Tramway Museum*

Despite a recent downpour a couple brave the upper deck of No 6 as it leaves Rhos Promenade on 15 May 1955. Built by UEC in 1914, it was the oldest 'Bournemouth' and was later preserved. *Ray DeGroote / Online Transport Archive*

In 1946 two 4ft-gauge 'Streamliners' were acquired from Darwen Corporation. Built by English Electric in 1936, they were the most modern narrow-gauge trams in the country and were soon dubbed 'Queen Marys' in their home town. Before entering service in Llandudno (where the fleet numbers, 23 and 24, were transposed) their maximum-traction trucks were re-gauged. The company hoped these 56-seaters would entice passengers onto their trams during the winter months, but unfortunately the Ministry of Transport refused to allow them to carry passengers over Penrhyn Hill in case strong winds caused them to topple over. As a result they were confined to operating shuttles at either end of the line, and no colour view of them in service has come to light. Fortunately, this view of 24 was taken on Brompton Bridge on 17 June 1951 during a tour organised by the Light Railway Transport League. *W. J. Wyse / LRTA (London Area)*

In this magnificent view recorded on 9 July 1955 'rack' 21 trundles sedately along Brompton Avenue as a Crosville bus heads for Llandudno. As the four 'racks' always faced in the same direction, the relevant terminus was painted on each dash, and a detachable enamel plate was also displayed. The 60 passengers were accommodated on 14 full-width lift-over bench seats plus two half-width flip-over seats either side of the trolley mast. The conductor collected the fares from retractable running boards. It is hard now to describe what it was like to ride on an open 'toastrack'; passers-by smiled and waved, and those on board enjoyed the breeze and the passing scenery. At the end of the 1955 season the 'racks' were placed in store awaiting the next season but they never ran again. What a tourist attraction the tramway would be today! *J. B. C. McCann / Online Transport Archive*

DUNDEE

STANDARD GAUGE, CLOSED 21 OCTOBER 1956

- Time-warp operation with single track and passing loop sections and trams retaining Edwardian complex lining-out
- 56 trams in 1950
- All routes converge on hub, radiating out to suburbs
- Closely-spaced tracks
- 16½ route miles
- Compact rush hours (less than 45 minutes!)

Dundee is (or, to be more precise, was) known as the city of the three 'Js' — jute, jam and journalism — but for this Edinburgh-born lad had to be added a fourth — jealousy. My introduction to the trams of Juteopolis came in the early 1950s, when the system presented such a vivid contrast to the seemingly staid system of my home city as to create an instant attraction. Instead of sombre, sober, maroon city conveyances, here were bright green-and-cream confections. In lieu of track almost universally double, here were multiple-line layouts in the city centre and single track leading tantalisingly off down mill-encrusted side streets; I was envious; indeed, jealous. Later visits showed three basic varieties of car — three-, four- and five-window — and awareness soon followed of the sub-species contained within that over-generous classification. The joys of longitudinal polished leather seating with ruby-red fanlights above were but adjuncts to the sometimes hair-raising descents from Maryfield or Lochee to the city.

A. W. Brotchie

The fleet

Five-window cars

Below left As a general rule of thumb the mix of three-window cars ran on the Ninewells–Maryfield route, the 10 four-window cars were confined to Lochee whilst the 18 five-window cars mostly plied from Blackness to Downfield. Like the Sunderland bogie cars of the same vintage these 18 trams underwent several metamorphoses. The two types, both delivered as open-top bogie cars, are seen in their rebuilt form in this remarkable May 1937 view. Major modernisation came during 1928-32 involving bodywork reconstructed as fully enclosed and mounted on new EMB trucks incorporating high-speed motors and improved braking. Nos 1-10 were built by the Electric Railway & Tramway Carriage Works in 1900, and 11-18 (formerly 41-48) by G. F. Milnes in 1902. Note the decorations for the Coronation of King George VI, the differences in the ornate liveries and the use of route numbers (discontinued during the War). By the early 1950s these cars were life-expired. When tenders for a new articulated single-decker proved too expensive it was decided to replace the Blackness–Downfield route in November 1955 on an experimental basis. This became permanent, and closure of the rest of the network soon followed. *OTA collection (photographer unknown)*

'Watty Young' cars — 29-33, 53-56

Above: The habit of naming particular classes of trams after general managers occurs quite often in these pages but was less common in Scotland. Whoever heard of a Glasgow 'Cunarder' being described as a 'Fitzpayne'? Dundee offers the only example — these were the nine fully-enclosed 'Watty Young' cars. Parts for these cars, which dated from the mid-1920s, were put together on an upper floor of the Lochee Road workshops and carried down a flight of stairs to be assembled. This may explain why they were diminutive (although undeniably neat). The first five had extremely short platforms, allegedly to *avoid* overcrowding; later examples rectified this fault to an extent. New as 91-99, they were renumbered in 1928 and again in 1936. When modernised the short cars were given EMB hornless trucks, as with 55 (originally 93 and later 79) at Maryfield Depot. This 1901 building still stands and is 'B' listed, although categorised by the Scottish Civic Trust as being 'at risk'. *Ray DeGroote / Online Transport Archive*

'Lochee' cars — 19-28

Supplied by Brush in 1930 these were Dundee's last and best trams. They had flush sides and were equipped with resilient 8ft 6in EMB trucks and high-speed 50hp motors. With seats for 62, they were the only cars with transverse seating in the lower saloon and upholstered seats upstairs. These flagship trams were actually intended for the prestige Ninewells–Maryfield service, but it was found two were unable to pass safely on the closely-spaced trackwork. As a result they were assigned to the Lochee service, and even there some clearances had to be enhanced. Ninewells' loss was Lochee's gain, but owing to its reputation as the 'Dark Suburb' there must have been anxious beating hearts (not to mention red faces) amongst Transport Department officials. This was the only route to terminate in the city, the cars using an anti-clockwise one-way city-centre loop. In 1956, 26 turns from Lindsay Street into Nethergate, with its attractive centre poles. The Steeple Church (left) is one of very few buildings not swept away by redevelopment. *J. G. Todd / Online Transport Archive*

Three-window cars — 34-51

Opposite Capable of working system-wide, these were the mainstay on the cross-town Ninewells–Maryfield route. Delivered from Hurst Nelson as canopied balcony cars between 1916 and 1921, they were rebuilt between 1928 and 1932 as 56-seat fully-enclosed cars with EMB trucks, high-speed 50hp motors and improved braking. Framed by a magnificent centre pole, 35 has just left Murraygate, now pedestrianised but still retaining its tram track, crossover and granite setts as part of the hard landscaping. The solid Clydesdale & North of Scotland Bank is at the junction with Seagate, from where the former independent Dundee, Broughty Ferry & District trams left for Monifieth until 1931. D. M. Brown's has long since departed the scene. This is one of many images in this book taken by a young American enthusiast who toured the UK's tramways in 1955. His day trip to Dundee was on 25 May. *Ray DeGroote / Online Transport Archive*

Tramway hub
All routes converged at the High Street hub which was also a major crew-assembly point. Movements through the hub, with its complex track layout, were controlled from the green telephone box by a duty inspector. To avoid delays, an avoiding track enabled Lochee bound cars to 'overtake' those at the kerbside loading points for Downfield and Maryfield. Conversion from trolley pole to bow collector took place between 1934 and 1936. On most of the routes there was a steady climb from the hub to the outer terminus. All principal car types can be seen in this overview. *Ray DeGroote / Online Transport Archive*

Taken from Reform Street, this side view of one of the former bogie cars illustrates the lower-deck longitudinal seating whilst the motorman has a padded seat like a shooting stick. When this view was taken the car was well over 50 years old. Today, City Square is still dominated by the Caird Hall which now has its stonework cleaned and restored. *Ray DeGroote / Online Transport Archive*

Blackness–Downfield
This cross-city route was replaced by buses on an experimental basis only in 1955 but it never re-opened. Well-to-do Blackness Road had sections of single track and loops and 13 is negotiating one of these sections while another tram awaits access at the passing loop in the distance. As in many other views, there is a complete absence of other road traffic. *Ray DeGroote / Online Transport Archive*

This was the extent of Dundee's reserved track — perhaps the shortest ever? No 8 of 1900 is collecting passengers from the loading island in the middle of the roundabout at Kingsway. The notice reads 'Tramway Station — No thoroughfare'. A traction power-feeder connects into the overhead, signalled by the disc with the letter 'S' on the span-wire. *Ray DeGroote / Online Transport Archive*

Ninewells–Maryfield
This was another busy cross-city service. The intensive rush-hour service along the prestige Perth Road survived to the end despite the growing use of private cars. Also the outer end of the Ninewells section was the last street tramway in Britain to be mainly single track with passing loops. *Ray DeGroote / Online Transport Archive*

On the other side of town, 35 has left the High Street hub and is climbing past solid suburban dwellings on its way to Maryfield. The tram-stop sign is hand-painted directly onto a red band on the traction pole. At this location, motor vehicles would have had no hope of passing the tram on the nearside. *W. G. S. Hyde / Online Transport Archive*

Lochee Route
At just over two miles this was the shortest route with grades of 1 in 11 and a three-minute headway during rush hours — always a tram in sight! The last car built by the Corporation passes Dudhope Park on the downhill run into town (17 minutes outbound and 14 minutes back!). These 58-seaters tended to be limited to rush hour, school and football special duties. *Ray DeGroote / Online Transport Archive*

Lochee regulars 27 and 28 stand at the terminus on 25 May 1955. By this time a simplified livery had been applied to a few cars. Despite a pressing need for economies, it still featured lining-out employing 'Greek key' corner patterns on the lower green panels. The lettering on the car side adjacent to the platform intimated the seating capacity. The glazed aperture below the upper indicator (here set to blank) had once displayed the route number. *Ray DeGroote / Online Transport Archive*

EDINBURGH

STANDARD GAUGE, CLOSED 16 NOVEMBER 1956

- Originally cable-operated.
- Major electrification did not start until the early 1920s
- Used twin coloured lenses for night time route identification
- Flew flags from trolley ropes during the Edinburgh Festival and other Special Events
- Used trolley poles with carbon skids
- Used re-wiring skates
- Incorporated former Leith Corporation fleet after boundary changes in 1920
- Purchased remainder of the former Musselburgh & District tramway in 1931
- Maximum fleet 360 cars
- 47½ route miles
- Unusual in operating some all-metal bodied cars
- New cars built until 1950

Below left Anyone who remembers Edinburgh's first-generation trams will never forget their coloured route lights which, at night, offered a kaleidoscope of colours as processions of cars paraded along Princes Street. Few night views exist, but in July 1956 this rare shot was taken of 234 at Granton Road Station on service 23 (green over yellow). *D. G. Clarke*

The lower saloons of Edinburgh trams had dark polished wood and shiny leather seats — or, if you were on one of the 'posh ' routes, a patterned moquette. Everything was clean and sparkling, and there were signs with the car number or 'FARE TABLES' in gold lettering. At night the trams were well lit inside, the older ones having the lamps in glass shades with wavy edges, while outside they gave a colourful show with red, green, blue, yellow and white indicator lights depending on their route. They were islands of bright light in even the best-lit streets. Our trams were warm and clean, speedy and smooth-running until the decision was taken to abandon them, after which they rapidly became shabby, and the track condition deteriorated. Even so, the streets were the poorer for their loss.

George Fairley

Below right Edinburgh did not introduce electric trams on a large scale until the early 1920s when the outdated cable-car system was replaced. As a result, scores of electric trams were needed of which some 80 came from outside builders while a further 125 or so were either converted from (or included parts of) cable cars, by the Corporation at its Shrubhill Works between 1925 and 1934. All had Peckham P22 trucks, seats for 56 or 58 passengers and, mainly, two 50hp motors. Although dating from 1934, 152 still had upstairs bulkheads originally part of the specification for earlier open-balcony versions built until 1929. With the Firth of Forth on the right, this is the Craigentinny Avenue terminus of service 19. Edinburgh's unique re-wiring skates introduced during the Second World War helped crews to connect with the overhead wire when turning trolleys during the hours of darkness. *Ray DeGroote / Online Transport Archive*

Wooden-bodied 'Standards'
Another batch of 10 cars, which entered service during 1932-33, had 56-seat fully-enclosed bodies built by R. Y. Pickering & Co, of Wishaw. One of these, 256, is seen eastbound on Princes Street in 1955. Note the provision of a slipboard providing additional route information. These came in variety of colours with the yellow board on 256 stating 'via Leith Walk'. The Corporation had built 13 similar cars at Shrubhill in 1929-30. Advertisements first appeared in 1952. *M. J. Robertson / Online Transport Archive*

Experimentals, 1932-34

No 180 was the first of a series of experimental trams placed in service prior to the introduction of the 1934 'Standard' cars. Built at Shrubhill for £4,000 (not cheap for a 1932 tram), it had ground-breaking alloy-framed bodywork. Its most distinctive feature was the original bright-red livery set off by grey window frames and silver lining edged in blue, which earned it the nickname 'Red Biddy' for the rest of its life, despite the livery being short-lived. This lightweight car had two 50hp motors and, for most of its life, a Maley & Taunton swing-link truck. Seen here on an enthusiast tour at Fairmilehead on 31 July 1955, it was the only non-standard tram to survive until final abandonment. Some of the half-drop windows look decidedly lopsided. *W. G. S Hyde / Online Transport Archive*

Two further flat-roof cars similar to 180 were built by Metropolitan-Cammell in 1933, but 260 and 265 had more angular all-steel bodywork with flat (as opposed to curved) glass. Note the folded up offside step onto the platform of 265. *G. G. Fairley / Online Transport Archive*

No 239 could be mistaken for a 1934 'Standard' car but was actually one of three steel-bodied 60-seat trams built by Hurst Nelson in 1934. These had domed roofs, whilst the seating and rounded ends resembled those on 180. Latterly the glass louvres over the half-drop windows had a tendency to fall out, as can be seen on the upper deck in this view at Granton on 31 July 1955. As the drawings for the 1934 'Standard' design had existed since 1932 one wonders if Hurst Nelson had been given sight of them. *W. G. S Hyde / Online Transport Archive*

Experimental Streamliners

Above In 1933 English Electric supplied the bodies for three domed-roof 'Streamliners' with sloping ends. With flags fluttering from its trolley rope, 262 is pictured in August 1955 in Lower Granton Road, the northern terminus for circular service 13, which was, in effect, an elongated figure of eight. *G. G. Fairley / Online Transport Archive*

1934 'Standard' cars

Left Various features from the experimental cars were incorporated into the final design of a new 62-seat standard car, of which 84 were built at Shrubhill between 1934 and 1950. During this period only a few alterations were made and all had Peckham P22 trucks, two 50hp Metro-Vick motors and BTH controllers. To the right of the tram is Register House while behind it is the since vanished FW Woolworth premises. In the foreground is a short length of cable track which survives to this day.
Alex Hamiton, courtesy Leo Sullivan

'Streamliners'

The only production cars following from the experimental group of 1933 were a further twenty cars of similar design from three different suppliers in 1935: Hurst Nelson (11-18); English Electric (19-24); Metropolitan Cammell (25-30). These were the last outsourced cars purchased new. There were detailed differences among the batches, the most obvious being the positioning of the route numbers and coloured lights on the Met-Cam cars. They also rode on a variety of different trucks. In May 1955 28 and 19 are seen at Craighall Road with the latter waiting access to the single-track section in the foreground. Right to the end the former Leith system retained a separate identity with its narrow streets, single-track sections and ornate traction poles. The lady on the right is extremely well dressed; no less would be expected in the capital, particularly on a Sunday. *Ray DeGroote / Online Transport Archive*

The 'Manchesters'

Although Edinburgh took over the Leith Corporation fleet as a result of boundary changes, it did not indulge in second-hand purchases; that is, until after the Second World War, when 11 'Pilcher' cars were acquired from Manchester. R. Stuart Pilcher had been General Manager in Edinburgh before moving to Manchester, so it is perhaps not surprising that when painted in Edinburgh's madder and white livery they bore a remarkable resemblance to contemporary 'native' trams. On arrival, the cars were subjected to extensive work at Shrubhill, which also had to be adapted to accommodate them. Entering service during 1947-49 they were longer than all other trams so were assigned to Portobello depot for routes 20 and 21. Having apparently been rejected by Aberdeen owing to its poor condition, Manchester 381 made its way to Edinburgh, where it became 411 and is seen in 1950 passing Portobello Power Station, opened in 1923; the site is now occupied by housing. This was among the last 'Pilchers' to be withdrawn, in the spring of 1954. *C. Carter / Online Transport Archive*

Princes Street
This was one of the great tram streets of Europe with its loading islands, centre poles and baskets of hanging flowers. The lines of stately trams seemed to fit in perfectly with their grandiose surroundings. By the time this photograph was taken in May 1955, the road surface was in shocking condition. Heading east, 89 passes the landmark Scott Monument on service 6 — the Marchmont Circle. Allocated to Tollcross depot, this 1933-built car was on borrowed time. The elegant silver-painted centre poles demonstrate one reason why bow collectors would not work in Edinburgh. In the distance the *North British Hotel* (since renamed the *Balmoral*) rises above Waverley station; traditionally its clock has always been set a few minutes fast to ensure train passengers arrive in good time. The tram-replacement Leyland PD2s did not find favour initially, being described as ' quivering masses of shivering tin'. On the left the SMT AEC with Duple bodywork was rather more luxuriously appointed.
Ray DeGroote / Online Transport Archive

West End
No 215 has just turned into Lothian Road from Princes Street, with Binn's department store prominent. Until 1954 trams had proceeded westwards towards Haymarket. To cater for the services passing this point staggered stops were needed, that for service 6 proclaiming 'Lothian Road for Princes Street Station'. Today the former LMS Station has gone, although the associated *Caledonian Hotel* still thrives. Later 1934 'Standards', like 215, incorporated ventilation louvres in the roof domes, along with quarter-drop opening windows. Note the difference in the shades of madder on the lower and upper panels. When Shrubhill overhauled cars invariably only the lower panels were fully repainted; if the upper panels were undamaged they would simply be re-varnished, which accounted for their appearing darker. *Ray DeGroote / Online Transport Archive*

Tollcross

The Shrubhill 'Standard' design was restrained but neat. Car 204 of 1937 and car 37 of 1949 have different types of opening windows. The track leading into Tollcross depot leads off to the right, and Howard & Wyndham's *King's Theatre* is on the left, beyond the cars. Bus 691 is actually older than 37, dating from 1948. Running on service 45, it is a Daimler CVG5 with Metropolitan-Cammell bodywork featuring the cut-away rear entrance common in many Scottish fleets. *Ray DeGroote / Online Transport Archive*

The Bridges

Photographed from a northbound car, 'Streamliner' 19 has just left the busy Post Office junction and is crossing the North Bridge with the eastern part of Waverley station sprawling beneath. The *Carlton Hotel* is on the left, across the bridge and opposite the offices of *The Scotsman* newspaper, which have since been transformed into the *Scotsman Hotel*. At one time the North and South bridges were used by as many as ten services, of which seven remained in May 1955. No 19 is at the start of a long climb to Liberton on service 7. At night a double-red aspect was displayed on this route. Glasgow experimented with night-time route-colour indicators on two of its trams, but the police authorities refused to sanction the showing of a red light at the front of cars, despite their never penetrating the red-light district. (Let it be whispered, service 7 did!) *Ray DeGroote / Online Transport Archive*

Leith Walk

Above Many of the city's wide streets were ideal for tramway operation and could have carried segregated tracks. By 1955, broad expanse of Leith Walk still comprised thousands of well-worn setts. The tracks entering from the left are from Picardy Place, while occupying the site on the far right is the *Playhouse Theatre,* now a major entertainment venue. In its heyday Leith Walk was a major tramway thoroughfare served by a constant stream of cars on some 17 services. 227 is heading north towards to a spot once known as 'the Pilrig muddle'. This was where passengers once changed from Edinburgh's cable cars to Leith's electric trams. *Ray DeGroote / Online Transport Archive*

Foot of Leith Walk

Centre On 23 June 1956, 233 of 1936 and 247 of 1937 negotiate the remains of the once complex junction at the Foot of Leith Walk, formerly served by 11 routes. Both cars are working on service 16 (Granton–Fairmilehead via Leith Walk), one of the last to go. On the right is the *Palace* cinema, while on the left a sign points to the *Gaiety Theatre* (1899); converted to show films in 1913, this reopened as a variety theatre in 1944 with Will Fyfe topping the bill. It did not outlive the trams. *Vernon Wood*

Lower Granton Road

Bottom Centrepiece of this June 1956 scene is car 35, now at the National Tramway Museum. The lady passenger is being helped to put a folding pram on to the front platform. An examination of this car today confirms that, after this photograph was taken, it was considerably smartened up and given a roller-bearing-axlebox truck. It was a late substitute for 225, the last to be built, which had been scheduled for preservation but was involved in a serious accident and was not considered cost-effective to repair two months before closure of the system. On the adjacent goods line serving Granton Harbour (now removed) is an ex-LNER 'J37' 0-6-0 locomotive. *Vernon Wood*

LIVERPOOL

STANDARD GAUGE, CLOSED 14 SEPTEMBER 1957

- Original cars imported from Germany and the USA
- Greatest reserved-track mileage in the country
- Impressive Pier Head terminus
- Maximum number of cars 744
- Route mileage 97
- Edge Lane Works designed for a production line for new trams
- Last new passenger tram 1942
- Last new extension 1944
- New works car built by City Engineers in 1948
- System completely intact in 1947

In the early 1950s I worked as a tram conductor at Green Lane and Edge Lane depots. By that time the remaining cars were reasonably modern, comfortable and could be fast, especially on the grass tracks. They were more congenial to work on than buses, as there was more room on the platform, and although trams had their own characteristic motion it was less stressful than the lurching of a bus, especially after a long shift. The fastest runs were always on the last tram returning to the depot. After midnight the recently relaid track in Green Lane allowed a bogie 'Streamliner' the opportunity to show its paces. As we approached a slight bend one of my drivers would shout 'Nurse the duck!' and I would grab the rope in case the trolley left the wires. The camaraderie and excitement of life on the trams was very enjoyable.

Brian Cook

Liverpool was noted for having 28 miles of segregated 'grass' track, the last section opening in 1944. City Engineer John A. Brodie had pioneered the construction of urban reserved-track tramways in the UK as an integral part of a new programme of relocating people from overcrowded inner-city dwellings to new spacious 'garden suburbs' which were to be served by swift, affordable trams running on segregated grass tracks located, wherever possible, in the middle of dual carriageways. This photograph taken at Oak Vale on 5 July 1957 shows part of the first section of reserved track, opened in September 1914 whilst the lines to the left were new in 1936 and provided a connection with East Prescot Road. *J. A. Clarke*

Pier Head

When redesigned in 1921 the area in front of the main waterfront buildings included three interlinked tram loops (north, centre and south), each with its own assigned routes. Every day thousands crossed the river by ferryboat, and, with trams lined up in orderly fashion, those making for the business and commercial districts simply took the first car in the queue. On a wet or cold day this exposed spot was often bleak and windswept, offering little or no shelter, and at high tide the Mersey occasionally washed over the river wall. The first view shows a line of cars on the south loop in May 1955 whilst in the lower view taken on 15 May 1950, Streamliner 903 is on the tracks connecting the south loop to the centre loop. In the background can be seen the north loop closed just months later in January 1951. As each loop was abandoned surviving routes were relocated. The final procession of 13 cars left from the south loop on 14 September 1957 to a cacophony of dockside hooters and ships whistles. *Ray DeGroote and C. Carter / Online Transport Archive*

'Priestly Standards'

Between 1920 and 1933 some 355 of these four-wheel cars were built by the Corporation. Named after the then General Manager, Percy Priestly, the design evolved with improved bodies, seating, trucks, brakes and motors. The first examples had open ends to both decks, but those built from 1929 were fully enclosed. Most early cars were eventually fitted with driver's vestibules, and some were rebuilt to match the later 'Baby Grands' in seating and equipment. Some had 20ft-long bodies and 10ft radial-axle trucks (one even stretching to 11ft 6in). These two 'Standards', one in crimson lake and cream and the other in the livery introduced in 1933, are seen in Ranelagh Street in 1938. Although much of the backdrop is still recognisable today, many of the buildings in the far distance were destroyed during the Blitz, to be replaced by less-imposing structures. *G. D. Parry collection*

English Electric bogies – 758-769

These 12 cars built by the Corporation between 1931 and 1932 helped improve the public's perception of the city's trams. They had seats for 70 with comfortable 2+2 transverse seating on both decks and were equipped with English Electric inside-frame 'monomotor' bogies, air brakes and remote control ready for multiple working. Between 1938 and 1944 nine were given new motors, improved destination displays and EMB lightweight bogies intended for use under Streamliners that were never built. Five were also fitted with more modern electro-pneumatic control gear and as such survived until March 1955. One of the latter, 766, is seen at the Pier Head on an enthusiasts' tour on 5 September 1954. *Roy Thomson*

'Priestly Bogies' 770-777

Between 1933 and 1937 Edge Lane produced some 250 modern bogie cars. When the first examples, 770-781, appeared in a striking new livery of olive green and ivory they were dubbed 'Green Goddesses' (after a contemporary film), and this name was then generally applied to all the modern fleet, although there were distinct groupings with individual names and characteristics. For example, 770-781 were also known as the '770'-class bogie cars or 'Priestly Bogies'. These 70-seaters had improved interiors and indicators (inspired by LCC No 1), rode on EMB London-style 'HR/2' trucks (usually referred to in Liverpool as 'heavyweights'), were powered by four 34hp motors and had direct control equipment. The first eight had flat roofs and No 772 is seen at Pier Head in June 1952. *B. C. Sexton / National Tramway Museum*

'Priestly Bogie' 778-781

The last four of the class had shallow domed roofs and were more obviously influenced by LCC No 1. No 779 is seen on South Loop in May 1951; in the background is a 'Priestly Standard'. Nos 770-781 were all withdrawn by the end of 1953. *W. J. Wyse / LRTA*

'Robinson Cabin Cars' – 782-817

Although influenced by LCC No 1 and Leeds' 'Middleton Bogies', these well-appointed cars differed in having 120° reversed stairs. They were named after the City Electrical Engineer, Percival James Robinson, who was given responsibility for the new fleet following the death of Percy Priestly. Entering service during 1933 and 1934, nearly all these heavy cars (18 tons) had the same trucks and electrical equipment as the '770' class. New features included concealed lighting, folding doors and a separate driver's 'cabin' complete with driver's seat. Nicknamed 'Cabin Cruisers' the last three were withdrawn in March 1955 and of these, 812, is pictured at Southdene on 13 March 1954. *J. B. C. McCann / Online Transport Archive*

'Marks Bogies' 818-867

These 50 cars entered service during 1935 and 1936 and were named after Walter Grey Marks, appointed General Manager in 1935. He dispensed with the driver's cab and reverted to the more conventional 90° direct stairs and sliding bulkhead door. He also introduced a 'via' indicator at either end (although in this view it has been plated over). Within the group there were variations in the controllers and motors, whilst the EMB bogies were divided almost equally between the 'HR/2' design and a new 'Lightweight flexible axle' type. Seen at Lower Lane on 13 March 1954, 867 was powered by four 27 hp motors and mounted on the 'Lightweight' style bogies. The last of this class were withdrawn in March 1955. *J. B. C. McCann / Online Transport Archive*

'Streamliners' – 868-992 and 151-188

The most distinctive cars to be built at Edge Lane were the stylish 78-seat bogie cars designed by R. J. Heathman, of which no fewer than 163 entered service during 1936 and 1937. Although the bodywork was similar, they rode on three different types of trucks with the majority running on EMB lightweight bogies. On 5 May 1955, one of these, 177, has just clattered over the crossing with the Line of Docks Railway situated directly under the structure supporting the city's legendary Overhead Railway. The track curving in from the right had been disconnected for many years. In the background can be seen the Mersey Docks & Harbour Building and one of the art-deco ventilation shafts for the 1934 road tunnel under the river. *W. G. S. Hyde / Online Transport Archive*

Some 45 'Liners' were on EMB heavyweight trucks, mostly an improved 'Jo'burg' variant. Here 953 negotiates the remains of a former 'Grand Union' (a double-track two-way junction linked on all sides by double-track curves) as it turns from London Road into Lime Street on 3 September 1955. All but a handful of the 'Streamliners' had four 40hp motors and Metro-Vick electro-pneumatic controllers. As late as 1955, a number had been refurbished. Since the photograph was taken the buildings on the right, including Burton's, have been replaced by a nondescript office block. The lower end of London Road was once home to many small bespoke tailors shops. *J. B. C. McCann / Online Transport Archive*

Colour views of the 'Liners' mounted on Maley & Taunton swing-link bogies are very rare. Originally intended to go under longer wheel-base 'Priestly Standards' the use of these trucks meant 918-942 were nearly a ton lighter than the other 'Streamliners'. Looking resplendent in a new coat of paint, 942 was photographed at Kirkby in June 1952. All but one of the 'Maleys' were included amongst the 46 cars sold to Glasgow in 1953-54. *B. C. Sexton / National Tramway Museum*

'Baby Grands' 201-300

Because the 'Liners' were heavier per passenger seat they used more power. As a result 100 cost-effective four-wheel 'Baby Grands' were built at Edge Lane between 1938 and 1942. Although only 3ft shorter, these 70-seaters were 25% lighter than a 'Streamliner' whilst carrying just 10% fewer passengers. They had 9ft EMB flexible-axle trucks, two 60hp motors and refurbished controllers from older cars fitted with EMB interlock boxes. Not as swift as the 'Streamliners', they also tended to overheat. Also as on the 'Liners', the bodywork suffered from water ingress as well as from long periods of neglect during and after the war. Interestingly, all 100 'Baby Grands' were never in service at the same time. By the time the last ones entered service two earlier cars had already been destroyed or damaged beyond repair. Major rebuilds continued until 1954. On 31 July 1955 two 'Baby Grands' are seen on one of the fine stretches of reservation serving the northern suburbs. These were the last type of car to run in the city. *D. G. Clarke*

Last new tram

Already responsible for laying and maintaining the track, in 1943 the City Engineer & Surveyor's Department also assumed responsibility for the works car fleet which, five years later, were painted two-tone grey and renumbered into the same series as Corporation steamrollers and dustbin carts. In 1948 a new rail-grinder was built at the department's workshops. The body and motor-driven grinding equipment were new, but the truck underframe and electrical equipment came from withdrawn 'Standards'. No 234 is pictured at Edge Lane Works on 14 May 1955. Attempts to sell this car to another operator proved unsuccessful. Also on view is rail-scrubber 287. Its body which was fitted in 1939 was the lower saloon of a former 'First Class' 'Bellamy' built in 1910. *Ray DeGroote / Online Transport Archive*

95

Above After the Second World War, the Liverpool system was totally intact but, like so many other tramways, it had suffered from war-time neglect. Post-war plans for a modern system complete with subways and single-decker cars were quickly forgotten and, in early 1948, the City Council voted to replace their trams by buses with the first abandonments taking place in the June. However, in the post-war period many miles of track were re-laid and scores of the more modern cars fully rehabilitated so that by the early 1950s the remaining parts of the system were in reasonable condition and could have formed the basis for a modern light rail network. Towards the end, maintenance again fell away and in 1955 the crew from one of the Corporation tower wagons was carrying out emergency repairs to the trolley-pole on 'Baby Grand' 263. This was destined to be one of the cars in service on the final day of operation. *W. G. S. Hyde / Online Transport Archive*

Opposite top Since the trams were removed, some parts of the city have changed beyond recognition with whole streets disappearing or being drastically altered. This is especially true of this area fringing the University where car 241 is seen in July 1957 picking its way through a partially fossilised junction. As Liverpool is a hilly city with many steep gradients, in several places inbound and outbound cars used different streets, a practise known in tramway circles as 'Cannon-hilling' after similar arrangements in Birmingham. In the background is Paddington, a steep-grade were the single track was used by city-bound cars only. In 1934, it had been the site of a fatal runaway when a car careered down the hill and overturned at the bottom. *J. J. W. Richards / National Tramway Museum*

Opposite bottom Today some once-busy city centre streets no longer carry through traffic. In 1954, 978 descends William Brown Street then a major transport corridor carrying trams and buses towards Dale Street and the Pier Head. On the right are some of Liverpool's great civic buildings. Trams last used this part of William Brown Street in November 1955. *D. A. Jones*

97

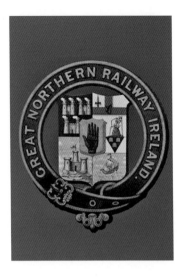

FINTONA

5FT 3IN GAUGE, CLOSED 30 SEPTEMBER 1957

- Branch line owned by the Great Northern Railway (Ireland)
- Last horse tram in Ireland
- Branch worked by the same vehicle for 74 years

After leaving the branch platform at Fintona Junction, the line curved gently to the left in a shallow cutting. Dick, the horse, plodded slowly between the rails along a cinder track which also served as a footpath. The pace was very leisurely and passengers who missed the car could easily catch it up or walk alongside chatting to the driver. Initially there was a slight downward slope but eventually the line levelled out passing through fields and by isolated dwellings before arriving at the goods yard at Fintona station. The terminal building had a covered roof and this is were the tram was stabled overnight. On weekdays, there some 10 return journeys sometimes supplemented by additional goods workings. Most lightweight goods was either carried on the tram's platform or in a small open 4-wheel wagon attached to the rear. Occasionally, a steam-hauled goods would also venture onto the branch. After the line closed, Dick retired to a nearby farm and the venerable tram was towed away for preservation.

M.Jenkins

Among the enthusiasts who journeyed to County Tyrone to photograph the horse tram which plied the GNR(I) branch from Fintona to Fintona Junction was Paul de Beer. On 10 June 1957 the lightly-loaded car leaves the covered station at Fintona at the start of its 3/4 mile journey. Goods traffic was still worked by steam locomotives. *Paul de Beer / Online Transport Archive*

Irrespective of gender, the horse employed on the branch was always named 'Dick'. So as to avoid being frightened by the steam locomotives, on arrival at the Junction Dick was taken into the small covered shed to the right of the signalbox. Dating from 1883, the tram itself was numbered in the GNRI carriage-stock series and had three classes of accommodation. This delightful time-warp passed into history on 30 September 1957. Fortunately 381 was preserved. *Paul de Beer / Online Transport Archive*

ABERDEEN

STANDARD GAUGE, CLOSED 3 MAY 1958

- Operated open-balcony trams until 1953-54
- Queen's Cross — last extension added to a first-generation tram depot
- Most northerly post-war system
- Radiating routes from main thoroughfare Union Street
- Maximum number of cars 118
- Approximately 16 route miles
- Featured distinguishing route colours until 1952
- Proponent of through-booking for bus feeder services to/from tram termini

From the sylvan surroundings of Hazlehead to the bracing breezes of Sea Beach, from the cosy congestion of St Nicholas Street to the varied vistas of the North Sea from King Street; from the rudimentary rows of Constitution Street to the gracious grandeur of Queen's Road; from the tall tenements of Rosemount to the majestic magnificence of Union Street and Castlegate, the lasting memories that persist are of sedate 'Standard' cars making their near-silent measured progress through the Granite City. Always experienced in a holiday atmosphere, the contrasts of the system with open-balcony cars running beside modern centre-entrance double-bogie vehicles; second-hand cars from two different origins; reserved tracks; single tracks with crossing loops in busy central streets; all, together, created a *pot-pourri* of interest. The route-colour bands on the 'Standards' and the sepia-tinted local views that decorated the upper-deck bulkheads only added to the pastiche that was Aberdeen.

David L. Thomson

The fleet

Open balconies

Although a number of colour views survive of Aberdeen trams in their final two years only a handful exist of the UK last open-balcony four-wheel cars. Seen at Hazlehead on 21 June 1951, 98 had a vestibule when new in 1921. It was originally on a Brill 21E truck but was given a Peckham P35 equivalent six years later. Powered by two 35hp motors, this 64-seat car was formerly allocated to the white Rosemount Circle route, but like other open-balcony cars it lost its dedicated route colour, becoming a spare car. An unusual feature of the livery was the cheerful vermillion-red paint applied to the truck, handrails and balcony seating — a welcome change from dull maroon or red oxide. The Hazlehead terminus featured a third track added in 1948 with a scissors crossover which helped to cope with crowds like these, but there were not many takers in winter. The last of these cars were withdrawn in 1954.
C. Carter

'Standards'
Between 1923 and 1931, 28 fully-enclosed 'Standards' entered service, ten being bodied by Brush and 18 by the Corporation. Two of the latter are seen on the narrow in-town section of Service 7 in this superbly atmospheric view taken on 29 May 1955. Nos 121 and 118 pass on the Schoolhill loop at St Nicholas Street. At peak times cars seem to be timetabled to the last second, so there were rarely any hold-ups. Latterly Service 7 was restricted to these rocker panel 'Standards' and the two modern four-wheelers. When on duty, the points-duty policeman here at Schoolhill loop was required to stand in the middle and breathe in as two trams passed. Eventually the 'Standards' were on Peckham P35 trucks. Both these cars were withdrawn following conversion of the 7 later in the year. *Ray DeGroote / Online Transport Archive*

'English' cars
Supplied by Brush in 1929, these 12 so-called 'English' cars had 66 seats, Peckham P35 trucks and two 50hp motors. Two are at Queen's Cross, where 129 is heading along Albyn Place to its Castle Street terminus whilst 126 is outbound for Hazlehead. They were not as tall as the older 'Standards', their straight sides allowing 2+2 transverse seating in the lower saloon for the first time. In earlier times the horizontal division of the upper-deck panelling had allowed a greater proportion to be devoted to displaying the route colour. The track coming in from the left provided access to Queen's Cross depot and formed part of the Rosemount Circle. Queen's Cross Church is constructed from granite taken from the nearby Rubislaw quarry. *Ray DeGroote / Online Transport Archive*

Experimentals

To assess the suitability of different types prior to placing a bulk order for new vehicles, four cars were delivered in 1940. Two (140/1) were 64-seat streamlined four-wheelers on EMB hornless trucks and powered by two 57hp motors. The highest numbered car in the fleet, 141 was also the last tram built by English Electric in Preston. Subsequent alterations included the fitting of longitudinal (in lieu of transverse) seating in the lower saloon. However, the most bizarre change involved replacing the original folding platform doors with van-type roller shutters that effectively denied the driver nearly all visibility to his right. Latterly, the two cars were regulars on service 7, and 141 in seen boarding passengers on the Great Northern Road on 29 May 1955. It was scrapped in 1956. *J. B. C. McCann / Online Transport Archive*

The other experimental cars were a pair of centre-entrance 74-seat 'Streamliners' (138 and 139) with EMB lightweight bogies and four 34hp motors. At the Transport Committee meeting that recommended their purchase it was claimed that 'the new vehicles are the last word in trams … They are the best yet made, ahead of Glasgow's Coronation trams', while the *Bon Accord* tabloid ran the headline 'Glasgow has nothing to crow about now'. When an order for 20 similar cars was placed after the war English Electric had stopped building tram bodies, so was pride swallowed when Aberdeen asked Glasgow Corporation Transport to build 20 'Coronation' bodies in their place? In the event this proved impossible, and the order went to R. Y. Pickering. On 26 May 1955 No 139 passes the Gloucester Hotel in Union Street, the most important business and commercial thoroughfare in the city. *Ray DeGroote / Online Transport Archive*

'Pilchers'

To keep the fleet up to date two batches of second-hand trams were acquired. Although not pursued with the same zeal as in Sunderland or Leeds, the purchases were judicious and considered, as befits the careful Aberdonian. No colour views have been found of 18 trams purchased from Nottingham in 1936, but quite a few exist of the 14 ex-Manchester 'Pilchers' which entered service between 1947 and 1950. Expecting (and probably getting) the best available, Aberdeen paid more for its 'Manchesters' than other operators. Major rehabilitation work included raising the height of the upper decks. The last to be withdrawn in June 1956 was No 49 which is seen at Hazlehead during an enthusiasts' tour in August 1955. To the delight of Mancunians in the party, the car developed the distinctive 'Pilcher' tail-wag when driven at full speed along the reservation. Plans to preserve one of these cars proved unsuccessful. *W. G. S. Hyde / Online Transport Archive*

Sea Beach

This sparkling scene captures the spirit of Sea Beach terminus, which on fine days thronged with holidaymakers when holidays at home were the norm. On 31 July 1955 Brush-built 'Standard' 112 of 1925 heads back to town on service 4. At times like this there was a constant stream of trams and buses, and at night they continued to serve the *Beach Ballroom*, just off camera to the left. *J. B. C. McCann / Online Transport Archive*

Bridges route

Above The city's premier cross-city route linking Bridge of Dee to Bridge of Don operated to a very frequent time-table and was the last to be abandoned. No 22 is seen at Bridge of Don, latterly the most northerly tram terminus in the UK. The Service 12 Balgownie bus connected with the trams here. When the folding doors on these cars were converted from manual operation a warning notice was inserted into the side panelling to warn motorists of the centre exit and alighting passengers. Although enthusiasts thought the' Streamliners' were wonderful they had limited route availability, high power consumption, required a three-man crew (when new) and suffered difficulties with snow and slush. The likes of Pirie's Confectioner & Tobacconist are typical of a bygone age, before supermarkets changed our shopping habits.
Alex Hamilton, courtesy L. Sullivan

Left Situated off the Bridge of Don route, the loop at Pittodrie was completed in 1937 to serve the adjacent football stadium (home of the 'Dons'). Heading this line-up on 19 April 1954 are 'Standard' 119. Wrongly displaying service 5, and 'Pilcher' 50. Until 1951 the route colours used to complement the service numbers were red, green, blue, yellow, white, brown and (at one time) black, the route-number displays being coloured to match. The route information and designated colour were at first confined to the upper side panelling below the main upper-deck windows but were later carried around the ends to be more conspicuous on approach to stops. The explanation for the wrong service number in this view would be to avoid the need to crawl under the front seat on the upper deck to change the screen!
J. B. C. McCann / Online Transport Archive

Above On 26 May 1955 a city-bound 'Streamliner' working in from Bridge of Don passes King Street depot and works. The buses in the yard were older than the tram and comprise a miscellany of pre-war and utility Daimlers and early post-war AECs. They would all outlast 33, which gave less than nine years' service. In the run-up to abandonment they were offered to Glasgow, which showed no interest, and were inspected by Blackpool officials, who considered them too slow. Slow — *in Blackpool?* Perhaps they feared the cramped saloons would slow loading and unloading of luggage-laden holidaymakers. They were probably right. In the event, they were all burned at Sea Beach. Such profligacy did not sit well with Aberdeen's reputation for being financially 'careful'. *Ray DeGroote / Online Transport Archive*

Right Among the 40 or so cars required for the 'Bridges' route were 18 'Standards' which were needed to overcome the shortcomings of the newer cars. No 114 is seen inbound along Holburn Street on the Bridge of Dee section on 26 May 1955. *Ray DeGroote / Online Transport Archive*

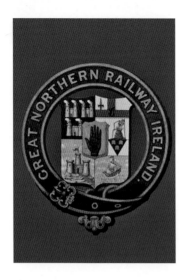

HILL OF HOWTH

5FT 3IN GAUGE, CLOSED 31 MAY 1959

- Last system in the Republic of Ireland
- Last 5ft 3in-gauge tramway in the British Isles
- Last tramway in the world operated exclusively by open-top double-deckers
- Last electric tramway in the British Isles worked exclusively by its original rolling stock
- Route mileage: 5¼
- Maximum fleet strength: 10 passenger cars
- Built by the Great Northern Railway of Ireland, ownership passing to the GNR Board in October 1953 and to the Road Passenger Section of Coras Iompair Éireann in October 1958

I first encountered the Hill of Howth trams when my parents brought me and my siblings by steam train to Sutton station, where we boarded the tram for the horse-shoe-shaped journey over the scenic hill and down to Howth harbour and station. This was a regular outing, and my love for these trams knew no bounds. We always sat on the upper deck at tree-top level, floating past some grand houses as if on a magic wooden carpet and then by fields of cattle and sheep to Howth Summit. The experience was completely different from travelling on Dublin's city trams. Instead of busy businessmen and shoppers and a grumpy conductor collecting fares, the Hill trams were packed with day-trippers, while a cheerful conductor whistled away as he punched the tickets. The city trams wore a sober green and cream livery and were covered from stem to stern with advertisements, but the Hill trams were a cheerful blue and white with large red lettering and were not demeaned by the vulgarity of selling products. The tram staff knew the regulars intimately, collecting meat from the butchers and papers from the newsagent for delivery to their favoured customers. One smart conductor would even do the sums for his student passengers. It was a fun system with a holiday atmosphere and a popular haunt for young lovers and happy families. Its tragic loss is still keenly felt by those who remember it.

James Kilroy

The fleet
Built by G. F. Milnes, 9 and 10 were designed for summer use by the GNR. Delivered in 1902, they were heavier, higher and longer than the Brush cars and had an unusual knifeboard seat in the lower saloon and two 40hp motors mounted outside the axles. As the pony wheels on the Peckham 14D-5 maximum-traction bogies tended to leave the track, for more than 55 years these 73-seat cars worked only on the Sutton–Summit section for a few days each season. However, after being fitted with cross-springs taken from withdrawn Brush cars they saw more regular use during 1958. On 11 August, No 9 is seen loading passengers at Sutton & Baldoyle station. Right to the end they looked particularly splendid in their grained mahogany (or 'teak') livery with the legend 'Great Northern Railway' picked out in gold lettering on the decency board. *Paul de Beer / Online Transport Archive*

Any views of works cars outside depot confines are comparatively rare. Howth No 11, which was mounted on Brill 22E bogies and built to carry goods traffic, was photographed on the line in 1958. In the early 1930s, it had been converted into an all-purpose works car and tower wagon. Latterly, it was often in action repairing damaged overhead or broken rail joints. *Paul de Beer / Online Transport Archive*

All the car types associated with the line are seen in this remarkable view taken inside Sutton depot on 11 August 1958. No 4 is in Oxford Blue and cream, the last of three liveries applied to cars Nos 1-8. Since delivery in 1901, these Brush-built cars remained the mainstay of the line. They had 67 seats, Brill 22E bogies, two 37 hp motors and air, hand and rheostatic brakes. Early on, the upper-deck railings were raised to prevent passengers from being struck by foliage or by some of the traction poles that had been positioned too close to the track. *Paul de Beer / Online Transport Archive*

The route

Other than at road crossings, the route was entirely on private right of way, with a mix of roadside and cross-country running. Here No 8 has just left the yard at Sutton and Baldoyle station on 13 May 1955 outbound for Howth. It is crossing Station Road which it will then parallel on reserved track as far as Sutton Cross, the former crossing point with the Dublin United route from the city to Howth abandoned in 1940. *Ray DeGroote / Online Transport Archive*

Out-of-season loadings were often light, the cars being used mainly by locals and schoolchildren. A simple signalling system controlled movements between the ten loops. At Baily Post Office the 'bull's eye' lamp is showing white, which indicated that the section ahead was clear. When the driver inserted a brass key to extinguish the light and the corresponding one at the other end of the section it was safe to proceed. *John Carlson collection (photographer unknown)*

Above A magnificent view of No 4 flanked by gorse bushes on the single-track grade between Baily View and Baily Post Office loops. To the right passengers could see Baily Lighthouse, Dun Griffin's Fort and the expanse of Dublin Bay. The steepest section of line up to the Summit was just over 1 in 16. John *Carlson collection (photographer unknown)*

Left A short distance from the Summit was the Baily View or Stella Maris loop, where No 1 is pictured waiting for a descending car to clear the section. Originally the line had several manned crossings, all of which had long since fallen into disuse. However, right to the end, the occupants of the house on the right (formerly the residence of a gatekeeper) were paid 1/- (5p) per week in their capacity as *ex officio* gatekeepers! *John Carlson collection (photographer unknown)*

It took 23 minutes to complete the climb from Sutton station to the Summit some 408 feet above sea level. On fine days this was a busy spot with through cars mixing with short-workings as so many people alighted here to explore the surrounding countryside. No 8, which last ran during the 1957 season, is seen on at the Summit on 13 May 1955. On these Brush cars, the two bogies were linked by 'cross springs' which prevented the pony wheel on the maximum-traction trucks from leaving the rails which enabled them to work over the entire line. *Ray DeGroote / Online Transport Archive*

To save money on electricity, cars on the Summit–Howth section often descended with their trolleys tied during daylight hours; at other times power was needed for lighting purposes. Here No 7 coasts through Offington Woods, just a short distance from Howth. *Courtesy Brian Greene collection*

In this timeless study of the terminal facilities outside Howth Station the crew of No 7 (motorman Peter Shiels and conductor Jimmy Conlon) prepare to leave for the Summit – journey time 10 minutes. When the use of the air brakes came to an end the constant application of the handbrake caused the bodies to develop this 'hog's back' or 'humped' appearance. All the Brush cars displayed 'Sutton – Hill of Howth – Howth' on the sides. During the 1950s the line suffered from increasing neglect. CIE didn't want it and thousands of day-trippers from Dublin no longer came by the trainload. Today, it would be a major tourist attraction. *John Carlson collection (photographer unknown)*

LEEDS

STANDARD GAUGE, CLOSED 7 NOVEMBER 1959

- Multiplicity of liveries
- Largest British operator of second-hand cars
- Extensive reserved tracks
- Suffered from political interference
- Complicated cross-city routeings
- Operator of Pivotal Truck cars
- Last regular use of four-wheel handbrake double-deckers
- Post-war plans for subways
- Last extension 1949
- Three single-deckers entered service in 1953/4.

All tram enthusiasts have a system that forms their benchmark, against which to measure others. Leeds is mine, for I spent my formative years there. I had seen others, such as London and Southampton, but Leeds in 1948 was a cornucopia of delights and interest. The trams were not doomed, and where else could you find the contrast between the 'Pivotals' and the ex-Hull cars with the trim 'Showboats', 'Lance-Corporals' and the super-speedy 'Middleton Bogies'? Liveries ranged from the traditional dark-blue and cream to more modern blue and finally the red era. A few cars which received special attention were given special liveries so they stood out. There were also second-hand cars galore and one of the most varied works-car fleets in the country, each type of car being numbered in a separate series. The variety exhibited by the cars also extended to their surroundings, back-to-back houses contrasting with every type of reservation, culminating in the off-road tracks through Middleton Woods.

David Packer

When Ray DeGroote stayed at the art-deco Queen's Hotel overlooking City Square on 19 May 1955 he took this heaven-sent opportunity to take this superb panorama from his bedroom window. Overlooked by the statue of the Black Prince, since 1937 trams had loaded in the centre of the square; however, as road congestion increased, special tram signals were needed. The cars on the right are inbound from Headingley, whilst the 'Feltham' is working across the city onto York Road. All three are in the final livery. The surrounding buildings are soot-blackened, women are wearing headscarves, and the men the ubiquitous gabardine raincoats. To the right, behind the trams, is Mill Hill Chapel. After trams stopped using the square in July 1956 the tracks in the foreground remained for access to the works until November 1957.

The fleet

'Hamiltons'

Many enthusiasts were attracted to Leeds by the different tram types and, after 1948, by the variety of colourful liveries. In his definitive history of Leeds Transport author Jim Soper confirms that there were more than 50 different livery styles. Over the years enthusiasts tended to name home-built cars after contemporary general managers; the 'Hamiltons', for example, were introduced by J. B. Hamilton, who during his term in office produced more than 130 trams, the last of which, dating from the period 1923-25, had Peckham P22 trucks and were the first fully-enclosed cars in the fleet. After being fitted in 1926 with air track, magnetic track and mechanical track brakes they were known as 'Beeston Air Brakes', after the steepest line in the city. Seen at Meadow Lane on 22 September 1950, 377 was destined to be withdrawn in 1952 and the last 'Hamilton' in 1955. *C. Carter*

'Chamberlains' or 'Pivotal' type

Some 200 of these cars entered service between 1925 and 1928, the majority having fully-enclosed 72-seat bodywork designed by General Manager William Chamberlain. All were mounted on 10ft-wheelbase EMB pivotal trucks, on which the pivoting axles were intended to give the riding qualities of a bogie car. Unfortunately there was insufficient interface between wheel and rail to allow the axles to be guided and pivot in the manner intended, and before long the trucks were 'rigidified', punishing the track as they squealed their way around curves. Moral: do not buy innovative designs in quantity straight off the drawing board. The bodies came from the Corporation (50), Brush (75) and English Electric (75). This view taken at the Corn Exchange in May 1951, highlights the layout of the pivotal truck under Brush 'Chamberlain' 32. The car is in the princess-blue and cream livery, with large shaded fleet numbers. The final cars with pivotal trucks lasted until 1954. *W. J. Wyse / LRTA (London Area)*

Above This is the south end of Briggate. In this thriving commercial thoroughfare were centrally-located queue barriers from which passengers boarded cars via the driving-end platforms. Movements were controlled by duty inspectors, and stops were staggered, each bay having a large route display, illuminated at night. On 19 May 1955 one of re-trucked English Electric 'Chamberlains' 142 is about to depart on service 1 to West Park. These were the first cars to have route-number boxes, but by now the lower aperture of the destination indicators have been painted over and the ruby glass quarterlights in the upper deck mostly replaced by plain glass. The last of this type was withdrawn in 1956. To the left of Horsfield 182 bound for Roundhay on circular service 3 is a Marks & Spencer's, a store which has become something of a national institution.
Ray DeGroote / Online Transport Archive

'Horsfields' 151-254
Named after R. L. Horsfield, these 104 trams, also known as 'Showboats', had six independent braking systems so could operate anywhere. The sturdy bodywork was a combination of emerging modernity, represented by flush sides, folding doors (added later), upswept dash panels, rounded glass and upholstered transverse seating, and traditional features, including ruby glass ventilator lights and flat roofs. Following four home-built examples, the production run of 100 was built by Brush during 1931-32 with Peckham P35 trucks of 8ft 6in wheelbase and two 50hp motors. Seen in Vicar Lane in 1951, 223 is in princess blue with large numerals, while the other 'Horsfield', in a simplified royal-blue version, lacks the cream bands below the windows. Significant numbers of these robust cars survived until final closure. *W. J. Wyse / LRTA (London Area)*

The arrival of the first ex-London 'Feltham' in 1949 coincided with a period of frenetic activity with experimental liveries, some of which were more successful than others and included all-red, red and duck-egg green and red and bright green. In 1950 the decision was taken to change from blue to red, and 226 is seen in a transitional London-style red and white, as befitted the orders of V. J. Matterface, Rolling Stock Engineer and a former London man. Eventually a darker BET red and white became standard. With two cream bands below the windows of each deck, this avoided cream-painted window frames, simplifying cleaning. *W. J. Wyse / LRTA (London Area)*

'Middleton Bogies' 255-271

Designed by Manager Vane Morland, Brush-built 255 of 1933 was admired by transport professionals from around the globe and, like LCC No 1, influenced the design of later bogie cars in Liverpool. It was also used for experiments with regenerative braking, but this was replaced by electro-pneumatic control as specified for the 16 production cars — eight each from Brush and English Electric, all with Maley & Taunton swing-link bogies, four 35hp motors, separate driver's cab, straight staircases, folding doors, 70 seats, twin headlights and a front destination display. In the first view English Electric 269 rests at Middleton on 15 September 1949, just weeks after the opening of Leeds' last tramway extension, visible in the background. The tram is in the pale-blue livery, with the coat of arms between the headlights and a stylised 'Leeds City Transport' on the sides, later replaced by the usual coat of arms and wings. All were later modified with single front indicators. *C. Carter*

This view taken in May 1951 shows one of the Brush-built Middleton bogies on the impressive high-speed, four-mile cross-country Middleton Light Railway, opened in 1925. The last of these fine cars was withdrawn in 1957.
W. J. Wyse / LRTA (London Area)

'Lance Corporals' 272-274
The nickname for these 1935 cars came from the 'V'-shaped stripes on the pointed ends of these trams, which were essentially four-wheel 60-seat 'Middleton Bogies' and were designed to attract people from the wealthier northern suburbs back to the trams. Internal fittings were luxurious and incorporated straight staircases and deep-cushioned revolving seats. No 272 seen here in May 1951 in the Matterface Royal blue and white livery. Originally nick-named 'Blue Bird' these cars featured the heavy roof guttering arrangement as on the 'Middleton Bogies' *W. J. Wyse / LRTA (London Area)*

The three 'Lance Corporals' rode on Maley & Taunton swing-link trucks. In 1952, 273 is seen in a later red and cream livery on the route they operated for most of their lives – the Lawnswood to Roundhay and Moortown Circular. All were gone by 1955. *W. J. Wyse / LRTA (London Area)*

Austerity car 275
This one-off was built to replace 'Chamberlain' 104, which was burnt out in 1942. For official purposes it was a 'reconstruction', enough materials having been found to build the nearest tramcar equivalent to a contemporary utility bus. The truck came from Llandudno, and the upper-deck wooden seats from open-balcony veterans. The interior layout was based on the 'Lance Corporals', albeit with a substantially reduced specification. Entering service in 1943, it was renumbered 275 five years later and is seen at Middleton in company with 'Horsfield' 197. It was withdrawn in 1957. *W. J. Wyse / LRTA (London Area)*

Post-war prototype 276
After the war Vane Morland produced a design for 50 double-deckers, but in 1946 post-war shortages made it impossible to secure tenders for new bodies, so second-hand vehicles were acquired as a short-term solution. However, in 1948 a sample car was built to test the design, which was a development of the Austerity car and the 'Lance Corporals', albeit greatly simplified and incorporating retrieved equipment. The last new tram constructed at Kirkstall Road, it is seen in Dewsbury Road in 1956, the year before it was withdrawn. The single-line destination display dated from 1952. *Harry Luff / Online Transport Archive*

Railcars 600-602

Plans for cross-city subways never materialised, but two very different testbed Continental-style single-deckers (601 and 602) entered service in 1953 in a special livery of royal purple and white to mark the Queen's coronation. They had 34-seat centre-entrance bodies built by Charles H. Roe with room for over 30 standees. No 601, which had relatively conventional equipment with EMB 'lightweight' bogies, is seen passing the Regal cinema on Hunslet Road on 19 May 1955.
Ray DeGroote / Online Transport Archive

'All Electric' 602 had the more advanced equipment incorporating Maley & Taunton Resilient Inside Bearing bogies and Variable Automatic Multi-notch Braking & Acceleration Control (VAMBAC) equipment, which suffered teething troubles similar to those encountered with Glasgow's VAMBAC 1005. It is pictured here in New York Street in June 1953, during the period when 601 and 602 were tried on virtually all routes. After trial service ended, both were banished to the short Hunslet route.
W. J. Wyse / LRTA (London Area)

In a reversal of their normal practice, Sunderland actually *sold* a tram in 1944! This was their No 85, a 1931 Brush-built single-decker which came to Leeds, where it was used for experiments relating to the projected subways. Then, in 1949, work began on converting into a railcoach. When it finally emerged in 1954, very little of Sunderland 85 remained, and the heavily rebuilt car incorporated many second-hand components. Here it rests at Hunslet terminus in 1955. All three single-deckers last ran in service in 1957.
W. G. S. Hyde / Online Transport Archive

Second-hand cars

Ex-London Transport 'HR/2s' 277-279
When war intervened just three of 25 'HR/2' cars scheduled to come from London actually arrived in 1939. The trio proved unpopular with staff, who found them very heavy to drive on the handbrake. Eventually 277 and 278 received air brakes and the latter is seen passing the *Clock Cinema* at Harehills on 18 July 1957 just months before it was withdrawn. *Paul de Beer / Online Transport Archive*

Ex-Hull works car No 6
No colour views appear to exist of the passenger cars acquired from Hull (some of which were nicknamed 'Kipper Boxes' by the Leeds staff) but, in a rare instance of a works car sale, Hull 96 became Leeds 6 and as such survived to the end. It is seen here on Sovereign Street on 29 June 1959. *Paul de Beer / Online Transport Archive*

Ex-Manchester 'Pilchers' 280-287
The seven 'Pilcher' cars acquired from Manchester entered service during 1946-1949 and one of these 285 is seen in Swinegate in the light blue and white livery it carried from November 1948 to August 1952 after which it was repainted in an unlined red and white livery. It was withdrawn in December 1953 just months before the last two 'Pilchers' in April 1954. *BC Sexton / National Tramway Museum Archive*

Ex-Southampton 'Pullmans' 290-300
The saga surrounding the purchase of the Southampton cars could fill a complete chapter. Suffice to say that only 11 of the 36 purchased were placed in service; some never left Southampton, while others were diverted to a pig farm, and those that did enter service only lasted for a short time. For example 298 only ran from 23 November 1950 to 5 June 1952. It is seen here in Swinegate on 25 August 1951 in its royal blue and white livery with straw lining on the dash and lower panelling as carried by most of the ex-Southampton trams. *C. Carter*

Two 'Southamptons' appeared in different versions of the red and white livery. 299 has a grey roof and upper white band with straw lining on the dash and lower panels. In Leeds, these trams carried a notice warning drivers that they were 8ft wide. This was the last Southampton to be withdrawn in October 1953. *W. J. Wyse / LRTA (London Area)*

Ex-LT Felthams 501-590

The first of 90 Felthams acquired from London Transport, 2099, arrived in 1949 and for sometime ran with its London fleet number and in London livery. Eventually, 83 Felthams entered service, the last in 1956. This rare view shows 'Oakwood Runaway' 507 a few months before it careered out of control along these same tracks, but in the opposite direction, eventually hitting Chamberlain 92 at 50mph on 4 September 1952. It was so badly damaged, it never saw further service. This is the early 'red dash' livery used before a broad white band was introduced below the cabin windscreens, improving their appearance. *W. J. Wyse / LRTA (London Area)*

Ex-LCC 'Bluebird' 301

Left This stylish car came to Leeds as replacement for two 'Felthams' lost in a fire. As Leeds 301 it only appeared spasmodically mostly operating at peak hours. On 18 July 1957, it passes through Sheepscar, months before it was withdrawn. Fortunately, it was subsequently preserved. *Paul de Beer / Online Transport Archive*

Left During the Second World War trams had played a vital role — scrapping was brought to a halt, and some routes were even reopened. At the time of the Suez oil crisis of 1956 trams were once again a valuable asset with some services being reinstated, for example in Leeds football trams were reintroduced to Elland Road. During the match cars occupied this long siding, which also gave access to Low Fields Road permanent-way yard, later used for scrapping trams. This view was recorded on the last day of football operation, 16 March 1957. One-way journeys to the scrapyard (left) finished later that year. No 217 was a GEC-equipped 'Horsfield' and these tended to be withdrawn before those with BTH equipment. Until the mid-1950s improvements were still being made to the 'Horsfields', including modifications to the indicators, fitting of sliding ventilators on the upper deck and substitution of electric for air bells. Latterly these required considerable effort with the plungers to achieve even a feeble ring to give stop and start signals to the driver. *Paul De Beer / Online Transport Archive*

This bustling, highly atmospheric city centre scene was taken in 1955 on Boar Lane, a principal east-west street which once carried a heavy concentration of trams. Horsfield 155 and Stores Car 8A share the road with Austin, Wolseley and Ford cars at a time when black cars were the norm rather than status symbols. 8A had started life in 1901 as an open-top double-decker. In its previous incarnation as Stores Car 5 it was grey and it did not acquire vestibules until 1954. Prior to this, it saw little use in cold weather but the wide open windows and absence of overcoats suggest that open platforms might not have been unwelcome on this occasion. *Alex Hamilton / courtesy Leo Sullivan*

SWANSEA & MUMBLES

STANDARD GAUGE, CLOSED 5 JANUARY 1960

- First passenger-carrying railway in the world
- From 1804 to 1960 operated successively by horse, steam, battery and electric traction
- Last complete tramway in the UK to be electrified in 1929
- Length: 5.38 miles
- Largest double-deck electric trams in the UK
- Lease held by bus operator South Wales Transport

In the 1950s the Swansea & Mumbles line became a much-loved television personality. When Glamorgan Cricket Club was playing at St Helens the commentator would observe: "… and there in the background glides the Mumbles train …". But was it a railway or a tramway? The original Act hedges its bets, referring to it as 'The Oystermouth Railway and Tramroad'! The protagonists for 'railway' will remind us of the bullhead rail, absence of street running, coal trains to Oystermouth goods yard and signals controlling the single-line sections. Tram enthusiasts highlight the unfenced nature of the line, its street-tramway voltage of 650V DC, ground-level loading and double-ended vehicles often operating in multiple. You must make your own choice.

R. W. A. Jones

The fleet and the line
This view shows the unprepossessing terminal arrangements at Rutland Street, Swansea with the depot and office on the right. Outside are two of the company's road vehicles. For the start of electrification, in March 1929, 13 Brush-built double-deckers were acquired. These 45ft-long cars (known locally as 'trains') had seats for 106, Brush equal-wheel bogies and two 60hp motors and at peak times could be coupled together, being equipped for multiple-unit control with continuous air brakes and pantograph collectors. The dark-red livery dated from 1935-36. *Ray DeGroote / Online Transport Archive*

The line

After leaving the Swansea terminus the first mile was along an unpaved, unfenced single-track section on the seaward side of Oystermouth Road, parallel to the railway from Swansea Victoria. On 27 May 1955 No 4 pauses at St Helens (The Slip), which until 1937 was also served by Swansea Corporation trams which terminated in the road on the left. The path in front of the London & North Western signalbox gave access to the beach. *Ray DeGroote / Online Transport Archive*

In the summer of 1959, No 3 pauses at Blackpill. In 1900 the original roadside trackbed was replaced by this alignment, which hugged the shoreline and eventually stretched all the way from Blackpill to Mumbles Pier. In the background is the main line from Swansea Victoria into Central Wales.
The imposing 1928 substation (left) was built for the electrification. *E. C. Bennett and Martin Jenkins / Online Transport Archive*

This portrait of a two-car train flanked by all manner of small craft captures perfectly the seaside nature of the line. In October 1959, the single-track section from here to Mumbles Pier was abandoned so that work could begin on converting the right of way into a road for the replacing buses. The green structure (right) was one of the electric signal boxes which controlled movements between loops. *Marcus Eavis / Online Transport Archive*

Although the line was mostly flat throughout, No 4 passes The Knab on the slight gradient up to Mumbles Pier, which was also owned by the South Wales Transport Co. *Phil Tatt / Online Transport Archive*

This view of the terminus at Mumbles Pier was taken in 1958. Because in places the track bed was only a few feet from the edge of Swansea Bay, the cars had air-operated folding doors on the landward side only. They also had 'dead man's handle' controllers, deep wheel flanges and air whistles. *Marcus Eavis / Online Transport Archive*

During the 1950s, the company allowed the infrastructure to deteriorate, and despite considerable local opposition the service, with its unique double-deckers, was withdrawn in 1960, bringing to a close 155 years of history. Today, there is considerable regret that the line was not preserved. *Ray DeGroote / Online Transport Archive*

SHEFFIELD

STANDARD GAUGE, CLOSED 8 OCTOBER 1960

- Only ever operated four-wheel cars
- Numerous steep gradients
- Last extension 1935
- Joint operation with Rotherham (ended 1948)
- Maximum number of cars 468
- Last new cars 1952
- Trolley reversers introduced 1915
- No trolley ropes
- 341 trams built in Queen's Road workshops
- Well-maintained, efficient system
- Last English city system to close

On 7 April 1947 I travelled by coach to the Sheffield United football stadium and saw convoys of trams in Shoreham Street. The object of my visit was to ride on the almost brand-new Jubilee tram, 501, which I knew was based at Holme Lane depot, so I boarded ex-Newcastle 314 for the short ride into the city centre, where I alighted near Angel Street. Here I boarded the first tram going west down Angel Street and on to Holme Lane Junction, where I got off. I did not have to wait long for 501 to appear. I boarded through the doors at the back and found a seat upstairs. The ride was smooth and quiet, very different from the ex-Newcastle car, and we moved swiftly through the city centre to Ecclesall Road Junction, where I descended and watched 501, in its cream livery resplendent among the older dark-blue cars, fade into the distance. I walked back to Shoreham Street for the coach to Bolton. I don't recall which team won, but I do remember riding 501!

Richard Wiseman

The Fleet

UEC or 'Preston' type
No 346 was from a batch of 15 open-balcony cars built by the United Electric Car Co in 1907. When rebuilt by the Corporation between 1924 and 1927 as fully-enclosed 62-seat cars they retained their Tudor-arch windows. Mounted on Peckham P22 trucks, they were all withdrawn by 1956, after which 346 served as a driver-training car until 1957. It is seen here outside Sheffield Midland station on 1 May 1955. *J. Copland, courtesy Martin Jenkins / Online Transport Archive*

Standard fully enclosed 'rocker panel' cars
Most cars built after the First World War bore a strong family resemblance as the Corporation progressively improved the basic design. Built at the Queens Road works in 1918, experimental car 366 was the forerunner of a fleet of 154 similar fully-enclosed five-window cars which entered service between 1919-1927 with bodies built variously by the Corporation, Brush and local firm Cravens, of Darnall. The distinctive 'banjo-shaped' bulge in the windscreen accommodated the swing of the handbrake. Here 366 ascends the steeply-graded High Street on 20 August 1951. This was a favourite location for photographers with the war-damaged shell of Burton's forming the background. This central area was heavily-damaged during the Blitz. *C. Carter*

One of the mid-1920s 68-seat Brush-built 'rocker panel, cars, No 53 waits among a number of football specials on Wolseley Road for the final whistle at the Sheffield United ground on 27 March 1954. *J.B.C. McCann / Online Transport Archive*

On 21 May 1955 Cravens-built 'rocker panel' 'Standard' 495 passes the University on its long climb to Crookes, the highest terminus on the system. All the 'rocker panel' 'Standards' had Peckham 'Pendulum' type P22 trucks, two 40hp motors and, eventually, air brakes. *Ray DeGroote / Online Transport Archive*

Among the last 'rocker panel' type to be withdrawn in 1957 was No 52 which is seen two years earlier about to pass under the Wicker arches on the main corridor out of town into the northern suburbs. In this all-electric vista No 27001 *Ariadne*, one of the locomotives built by BR for the 1954 electrification of the Manchester–Sheffield service, pulls out of Sheffield Victoria station closed in 1970. *Ray DeGroote / Online Transport Archive*

Flat-roof 'standards'
In 1927 Cravens built a car which became the basis for 210 straight-sided, five-window, 61-seat flat-roof Standards built between 1928 and 1936. All had Peckham P22 trucks and two 50hp motors. In May 1955, one of Corporation-built flat-roof Standards, 163, progresses along Fargate with the *Sheffield Telegraph* building in the background. *Ray DeGroote / Online Transport Archive*

Here passengers alight from the off-side of flat-roof Standard 198 in Market Place on 20 August 1951. This was one of 31 cars built at Queens Road in 1934, the highest number in any given year, and the last to enter service in the Prussian blue and white livery with gilt lining and large shaded fleet numerals. After 1936 a new cream livery with three azure blue bands was introduced. *C. Carter*

Twenty-five flat roof Standards were built by W. & E. Hill, of South Shields and one of these, 155, is seen ascending Commercial Street in April 1956. Sheffield's second-generation tram system again uses this thoroughfare. *Jack Batty / Online Transport Archive*

Domed-roof 'Standards'
The next 67 well-proportioned 'Standards' built at Queens Road between 1936 and 1939 had the same basic equipment as the earlier examples but differed through having domed roofs, straight sides and rounded features and were amongst the most stylish new four wheel trams produced during the 1930s. One of the class crosses Hillfoot Bridge in 1958, with the Neepsend Tavern, gasholders and distant hills in the background. *Marcus Eavis / Online Transport Archive*

As a major industrial centre, Sheffield suffered severe damage during the war, and 14 trams were destroyed. These were replaced between 1941 and 1944 by domed-roof cars. One of this group of 'Blitz' cars, 112, is seen at Fitzalan Square in 1958. Although many services were cross-city, some terminated at various points in the centre, including Fitzalan Square which was, with its covered shelters and underground enquiry and inspector's office, the operational hub of the undertaking. Initially, route letters were used but latterly the indicators only carried a limited amount of information which could, owing to the wide variety of additional peak time industrial services, be confusing for visitors. *Marcus Eavis / Online Transport Archive*

Looking very spruce in their attractive cream and blue livery, two domed roof Standards 251 and 236 pass on the High Street on 20 August 1951. These cars had five half drop windows on each side of the upper saloon but problems with the mechanism on earlier cars like 236 led to the provision of wind-down handles on 251. Sheffield constantly upgraded its trams in order to provide a first-class service. A number of this type of remained in service until the end. *C. Carter*

The Roberts cars

Above To commemorate 50 years of municipal operation the Corporation built a new luxury four-window 'Jubilee' car in 1946. Seating 62 passengers, it had a Maley & Taunton 9ft-wheelbase hornless-type truck, two 65hp motors and maximum braking efficiency; it was also the first Sheffield car to have fluorescent lighting, platform doors and no internal bulkheads. Still committed to tramway retention, a production run of 35 similar cars was ordered from Charles Roberts & Co. However, by the time the last of the group was delivered in 1952, the decision had been already been taken to scrap the system, so these handsome cars ran for only a few years. They differed from 501 in having all-metal bodies and a revised window arrangement at the ends of the upper deck. Sparkling in the sunshine, 527 was virtually brand new when photographed on 20 August 1951. *C. Carter*

Second-hand cars

Left and opposite The 10 cars acquired from Bradford were built by English Electric after the First World War. In Sheffield, they were allocated the fleet numbers 325-334. Before entering service, they were re-gauged and given totally enclosed balconies. Distinguished by their Bradford-style angular dashes, they ran in a war-time grey-green livery but sadly no colour views seem to exist of them in passenger service but after they were all withdrawn in 1951 one of them, 330, was cut down and converted into a railgrinder. In the first view, the works car is seen making its last-ever trip through the streets of Sheffield en route to Tinsley depot on 7 October 1960. In the second view taken some nine years earlier in August 1951, the newly converted car is seen on the High Street flanked by two Flat-Roof Standards. It is now preserved at the National Tramway Museum. *E.C. Bennett and Martin Jenkins / Online Transport Archive and C. Carter*

Above In urgent need of additional wartime capacity, Sheffield acquired 24 second-hand cars of which 14 came from Newcastle. On arrival these were transformed into fully enclosed cars at Queens Road Works and given the numbers 311-324. Amazingly, one was captured in colour and is seen in the background of this view taken on The Wicker on 17 September 1949. Built by Hurst Nelson in 1901, they had wooden seats throughout and, having no front indicator, this example carried an 'SCT' motif instead. All were withdrawn by 1952. *C. Carter*

The green revolution
As the predominantly-cream livery was costly to maintain, 23 cars appeared in green during 1952, but following a public outcry they were swiftly repainted. If only the outcry against the tram-scrapping programme could have produced a similar reversal! Wearing the two-tone version of the new livery, 76 boards passengers on the High Street and is followed by a newly delivered Roberts car in August 1952. *W. J. Wyse / LRTA (London Area)*

Eleven trams including 'Blitz' replacement car 83 were painted in one shade of green. Here it departs Fitzalan Square with one of many branches of the Yorkshire Penny Bank on the right. In the background is the experimental Standard 370 of 1931 which was unique in having aluminium bodywork. *W. J. Wyse / LRTA (London Area)*

Steep hills

A preponderance of steep gradients coupled with the tight curvature of the tramway prevented the use of bogie cars as well as restricting the overall length of the cars. Some of the steepest sections were on the Walkley route which featured a maximum grade of 1 in 10.7. Here 453 surmounts the famous Barber Road 'hump', with a Board of Trade regulation stop on the left shortly before this hilly route closed in April 1956. *Jack Batty / Online Transport Archive*

In 1959, domed-roof Standard 231 bites into the steeply-angled curve at Stubbins Lane corner on its way to Sheffield Lane Top. The curve on the inbound track (left) was so sharp the overhead wiring had to be off-set some distance from the track. This section was abandoned in April 1960. To provide additional revenue, adverts were reintroduced in 1952. *E. C. Bennett and Martin Jenkins / Online Transport Archive*

Trolley reversers

These were a major feature of the Sheffield system and obviated the need for conductors to walk into the middle of busy roads to swing the trolley. Car 72 is using the reverser at Wadsley Bridge in 1959. Both these cars were among 23 flat-roof Standards to have their lower saloons rebuilt between 1952 and 1956. *E. C. Bennett and Martin Jenkins / Online Transport Archive*

GRIMSBY & IMMINGHAM

STANDARD GAUGE, CLOSED 1 JULY 1961

- Light railway owned and operated successively by the Great Central Railway, the London & North Eastern Railway and British Railways
- Worked entirely by bogie single-deckers — the longest single-deck trams in the UK
- Last first-generation English tramway to close

This was a fascinating railway-owned tramway with cars from Newcastle and Gateshead being added to the original Great Central bogie cars after the war. The original long bogie cars had a central area for carrying bicycles and dock workers would smoke and playing cards in the saloons. At peak times convoys of green trams ran parallel to long steam-hauled goods trains. At night railway-uniformed staff would allow enthusiasts to drive the hourly solo car under instruction, with the single headlamp above our heads picking out the occasional rabbit.

E. C. Bennett

The fleet
Opened by the GCR in 1912 to transport the labour force from Grimsby to and from the new dock at Immingham, the line employed two types of single-decker built between 1911 and 1915, all having Brush bodies and equal wheel bogies. Twelve of these were the longest single-deckers in Britain, being 54ft 2in over the fenders, and were powered by two 50hp motors. It is believed that Nos 13-16 were ordered from Brush but completed by the GCR at Dukinfield. Two of the 'long' cars are seen here at Corporation Bridge on 21 May 1955. No 11 wears the green livery applied to all BR electric multiple-units and also sports the BR lion-and-wheel emblem, whilst No 1 retains LNER brown. To the left, with the sign still in LNER colours, are the waiting room and parcels office. *Ray DeGroote / Online Transport Archive*

The four short cars (5-8) saw relatively little service. They were acquired for proposed operation into central Grimsby which never materialised, and all were withdrawn in 1955, but No 5 was used subsequently as a works car until replaced by one of the ex-Gateshead trams. It is seen here in the vicinity of Pyewipe depot. *W. J. Wyse / LRTA (London Area)*

Centre The GC cars, which spent virtually their entire life out of doors, had wooden seats for 64 plus an additional tip up seats for eight in the central luggage compartment. No 1 is at the Tramway Station at Corporation Bridge. The lift bridge which crossed the dock in the background was designed to carry trams but tracks were never laid. Throughout, the day and night, hundreds of workers would congregate here ready to board the procession of trams waiting to take them, often in convoy, along the line to Immingham Docks. *Ray DeGroote/Online Transport Archive*

Second-hand cars
To meet the demands of increased post-war ridership generated by the establishment of new industries along the Humber three bogie single-deckers were acquired in 1948 from Newcastle Corporation (see page 25), but these were withdrawn following the acquisition in 1951 of 14 cars from the Gateshead & District Tramways Co. Not entirely successful, these maximum-traction cars tended to appear at peak times only, and in this scene, recorded in September 1958, 17 (formerly Gateshead 57) has just arrived back at Pyewipe. Note that the crew are wearing full BR uniforms. At this time as many as 19 trams were needed at shift-change times. The depot consisted of a number of exposed sidings and a small covered repair facility. *E. C. Bennett and Martin Jenkins / Online Transport Archive*

One ex-Gateshead tram was converted into a general purpose work car and given the BR District Engineer's number DE320224 — making it the highest-numbered tram in the UK. Towards the end, it was in almost daily use and is seen here on 3 May 1959 attending to the overhead at Immingham Town, accompanied by its mobile tower wagon. *Paul de Beer / Online Transport Archive*

The line
For much of its length the 7-mile line ran on sleeper track across flat, windswept terrain and paralleled a main-line railway which also served Immingham Docks. However, at the Grimsby end there was a mile of street running, with single track and loops which was abandoned in 1956 when the line was cut back from Corporation Bridge to Cleveland Bridge, where connecting buses were provided, although many workers opted to arrive by bicycle. Still in LNER brown with gilded fleet numerals, No 1 roars along the badly worn rails on 21 May 1955 when advertisements were everywhere, local shops were flourishing and a delivery boy's bicycle is parked against the kerb. *Ray DeGroote / Online Transport Archive*

Above Between Pyewipe and Immingham Town there were two passing places controlled by colour-light signalling. Boarding facilities were absolutely basic. These two cars are passing at Kiln Lane, Stallingborough, their powerful headlights being required to illuminate the right of way after dark. *Marcus Eavis / Online Transport Archive*

Left At Immingham Town there was a complex track layout as cars from both directions had to reverse before proceeding to their respective termini. On arrival, crews changed ends and also raised and lowered trolleypoles. At peak hours it was quite a sight to see as many as a dozen cars arriving and and departing within minutes of each other. In this semi-rural scene, recorded on 21 May 1955, a few local passengers have alighted, and car 14 is almost ready to leave for 'the dock'. The line suffered a slow, lingering decline. After closure of the in-town section at the Grimsby end the all-night service was withdrawn, and then, finally trams appeared only at peak hours. The replacing buses had to make a lengthy detour, almost doubling the journey time. *Ray DeGroote / Online Transport Archive*

GLASGOW

4FT 7¾IN GAUGE, CLOSED 4 SEPTEMBER 1962 (CLYDEBANK 6 SEPTEMBER 1962)

- Largest city operator in the UK outside London
- Largest municipal tramcar builder
- Colour bands — blue, green, red, yellow, white — used to identify routes
- Extensive services beyond the city boundary
- Maximum mileage 259
- Gauge enabled standard gauge railway wagons to share tramway track
- Purchased two neighbouring company tram systems
- Bow collectors introduced 1928-34
- Last extension 1949
- Maximum number of cars – 1208 in 1947
- All-female crews
- Last use of traditional four-wheel double-deckers
- Last city system in the UK
- Last Scottish city system to close

They had an audible and visual presence in our lives from our first awakening in the morning until lulling to sleep at night. To us youngsters they were the most natural things in our world, those large, friendly cars which commanded the prime position in the centres of our streets, garnering the city together. They were Glasgow. They were as the wardrobe was to Narnia — a medium to explore our native city, providing a seemingly endless recreation, a comprehensive education, a fulfilling pastime in a cheap, convenient way — a route through to an exciting world outwith the confines of home and school. From the safety of the top deck we could explore unknown areas, expand our knowledge of familiar quarters, all the time secure in the familiar environment of the electric tram. They contributed more than we realised at the time in the moulding of our formative years.

David L. Thomson

The fleet

'Standard' trams
More than 1,000 of these cars were built, and all but 80 were products of the Corporation Car Works at Coplawhill. These legendary trams were constructed to the highest specification, and with successive upgrading some almost spanned the life of the system, but their very longevity eventually became their undoing. They fell into two basic groups, the oldest being those with round dashes which were built from 1898 to 1909. First-build round-dash 'Standard', 751, which entered service in 1900 as an open-top, non-vestibuled car was progressively modernised and as such was the longest-lasting, continuing in front-line service until June 1960. This probably because it was given one of 10 EMB hornless trucks purchased in 1934-35, which were forgiving to the bodywork. It is seen in Argyle Street passing the *Adelphi* Hotel, located above Boots the Chemist.
D. E. Sinclair / STTS collection

The second basic group of 'Standards' were those with hexagonal dashes, built between 1909 and 1924, one of which 22 is pictured some 200 yards from the short terminal stub in Main Street, Cambuslang, a route which was always a preserve of the Standards. The buildings on the right once overlooked the interchange point onto the Lanarkshire Tramways and are still extant. Latterly most of these 59-seat 'Standards' were on 8ft-wheelbase trucks and powered by two 60hp motors, making them lively performers with the very last survivors being withdrawn in June 1961. When Jack Wyse photographed 22 in 1956 he could have had no inkling that it would eventually become a royal celebrity. Not only was it preserved and restored to 1920s condition as a white car; it also operated on the Glasgow Garden Festival tramway in 1988, conveying all the VIPs, including the Prince and Princess of Wales. Today, this is among several Glasgow cars at the National Tramway Museum. *W. J. Wyse / LRTA (London Area)*

'Kilmarnock Bogies' 1090-1140

Bottom There was a brief interlude after construction of the last 'Standards' before the first new 68 seat 'Standard Double Bogie' cars appeared. Although Coplawhill built a prototype in 1927, for rapid delivery, the Corporation accepted tenders for a total of 50 trams supplied by three outside builders. Delivered during 1928-29, they were usually known as 'Kilmarnock Bogies' after the Kilmarnock Engineering Co, which allegedly constructed the maximum-traction bogies. These soon proved prone to de-railing, finding little compatibility with Glasgow's pointwork despite successful operation elsewhere. As a result they became route-bound to the straight, flat east–west services from Clydebank to Glasgow's East End. Equipped with two 60hp motors, they had extremely resilient riding qualities, although performance was a little ponderous. R. Y. Pickering-built 1125 is seen at Bridgeton Cross on 23 May 1955. *Ray DeGroote / Online Transport Archive*

'Coronations' 1141-1292

While Liverpool progressed from traditional standard trams to modern streamliners in a measured process, Glasgow took 'one giant leap for tramkind'. Even as the last 'Standards' were being modernised, two prototype ground-breaking saloon trams were on the drawing board in 1935, the first,1141, appearing within a year. The second, 1142, differed from the production 'Coronations' in having a five-window saloon and Maley & Taunton equal-wheel bogies. When new it sported a special livery of red, silver and blue to celebrate the coronation of King George VI, becoming known as the 'Coronation' car, hence the name given to the entire class. A production batch of 150 cars entered service between 1937 and 1941. These impressive cars had platform doors, a separate driver's cab, curved roof lights, EMB bogies and four 35hp motors. They also appeared in a new livery of green, cream and orange. Still with its original visor and without the later small upper deck front window, 1229 passes two cinemas in Coatbridge in September 1956. Following the Glasgow takeover the Coatbridge system was connected to the main network by a roadside reservation, opened in 1923 and closed in November 1956. Many 'Coronations' survived to the end. *Ray Bicknese / Online Transport Archive*

'Lightweights' 6,1001-1004

By 1938 General Manager R. F. Smith wanted to make better use of modern equipment that was barely four years old yet allocated to 40 year-old 'Standards'. The result was five experimental economy 'Lightweight' trams, with a range of different equipment, that emerged from Coplawhill between 1940 and 1943. However, the Second World War thwarted any further development, and the 'Standards' carried on. Unloved by staff, being 'different', the 'Lightweights' were housed at Elderslie depot from 1951 until 1957. Although they were usually confined to rush-hour extras, 1003 is seen in all-day service at Paisley Cross in June 1956. All were withdrawn by 1959. *J. G. Todd / Online Transport Archive*

Single-ended tram 1005
In the UK, Vambac-equipped trams are usually associated with Blackpool, although Leeds and Glasgow had one each, the latter having the only double-decker example. Built in 1947, No 1005 had its control equipment slung under the rear platform, which layout effectively precluded the fitting of lifeguards and thus restricted it to unidirectional working. A separate entrance and exit was tried, and to ensure passengers recognised it was 'different' it wore this special livery, earning it the nickname 'Bluebird'. However, the public struggled to come to terms with its unusual layout, and the equipment also proved troublesome. A young Michael Waller obtained permission from the Corporation to take colour views of selected cars at Newlands Depot in May 1949 including 'Bluebird' which was then in broadly original condition. Later it would converted to conventional layout, control and livery. *M. H. Waller, courtesy Peter Waller*

Another 'one-off', 1089, represented an attempt to provide a high-speed inter-urban car. Dating from 1926, it had, like 1005, been unsuccessful in terms of its separate entrance/exit arrangements, and it was soon put out to graze on the Duntocher route. Latterly, it was used a crush-load shipyard extra and is seen returning to Partick depot on 23 May 1955. *Ray De Groote / Online Transport Archive*

'Cunarders' 1293-1392

Despite being operationally unsuccessful No 1005 was the precursor of the post-war 'Coronation Mk II' class. Usually known as 'Cunarders', these had Maley & Taunton inside-framed bogies and four 36hp motors, but stability issues took a little while to resolve, and these handsome trams were less popular than their pre-war sisters. Nonetheless, the 100 cars built at Coplawhill between 1948 and 1952 exceeded the total of all other new post-war trams built elsewhere in the UK. Newly-painted 1304 is seen in Renfield Street in its final livery, passing 1337 in an intermediate style. Examples survived until final closure. *W. J. Wyse / LRTA (London Area)*

'Goddesses'

Glasgow had a high-speed fleet! Even 'Standards' with their two 60hp motors could keep pace with the modern cars. Despite impressions that they might, like Milan's 'Peter Witts', 'go on for ever', judicious scrapping commenced after 1948, when trolleybuses and the 'Cunarders' were introduced. To release further veterans for scrap Glasgow acquired 46 Liverpool 'Streamliners' during 1953-54. At £500 each these seemed a bargain, but it soon became clear that they were suffering from the rigours of war and subsequent neglect, only partially remedied by later refurbishment. Nonetheless, they looked striking in Glasgow livery and proved fast given the chance. On 23 May 1955, 1034 (ex-Liverpool 885) is on service 29 in Argyle Street, about to pass beneath Glasgow Central station. The last 'Goddess' was withdrawn in 1960. *Ray DeGroote / Online Transport Archive*

Tramcar builders par excellence

Glasgow's car works is set apart. Over the years it constructed over 1,250 trams — more than any other operator. As late as 1949 repairs staff exceeded 3,420 men and women, most of whom were based at Coplawhill, with its electrical and body-repair shops, sawmill, foundry and blacksmiths, as well as an area for sheet-metal fabrication. An undiminished *esprit de corps* existed among the staff. Perhaps it was *'esprit de caur'* in view of the Glaswegian pronunciation of 'car'? Owing to slow-speed film, quality interior shots are uncommon. In 1958, 76 was in for bodywork strengthening. The cars were designed for ease of maintenance and accident repair. *J. J. W. Richards*

Originating when illiteracy was rife, the coloured route-band system, to differentiate services, lasted until 1952, with 'bus green' displacing the range of colours. Although Glasgow is one of the most photographed of all the UK tramways, much is owed to Clarence Carter and Jack Wyse, whose early endeavours feature the coloured route bands. In the first view taken in May 1951, 393 (1905-57) works the 'yellow' service through the West End and is seen at Botanic Gardens on Great Western Road. In the second view, 486 (1903-58) is on 'red' service 13 in 1951 at the Cowcaddens junction with West Nile Street, where all the buildings to the rear have gone, along with Buchanan Street railway station (just off camera to the right). Unlike 393, 486 would be repainted as a 'bus green' tram before acquiring side advertisements. *W. J. Wyse / LRTA (London Area) and C. Carter / Online Transport Archive*

During Coplawhill's final years forgotten talents were resurrected when several preserved trams were beautifully restored, some appearing in the former route colours, for example 1088 is in the old Prussian blue. When the Works closed the paint shop became Glasgow's first transport museum.
D. E. Sinclair / STTS

Argyle Street
Until June 1961 this trunk east–west corridor through the centre of the city, which once had nose-to-tail lines of cars and queues of people waiting to board, was the last major city street in the UK served exclusively by trams. One of the Pickering-built 'Kilmarnock Bogies', 1126, is at the junction with Buchanan Street in 1955. The characteristic lean associated with these cars is clearly shown in this early-closing-day scene, with shops' shutters pulled down. Observe the gent with his bowler hat and rolled brolly. The last 'Kilmarnock Bogies' were withdrawn in 1961.
W. J. Wyse / LRTA (London Area)

In this atmospheric scene crowds spill into the roadway to board the approaching 'Coronation'. Such mid-road boarding was one of the drawbacks associated with trams (at least, as today's Health & Safety culture would see it). By now most of the remaining cars are looking dingy and unkempt.
Ian Stewart

Above When the Corporation took over the Airdrie & Coatbridge Tramways (1921) and the Paisley District Tramways (1923) it also absorbed their fleets. From 1925 until 1959, former Paisley car, 1017, operated as a driver-training car and is seen here in September 1958 filled with recruits on short section of track close to Coplawhill works which was used for this purpose. This little car is now preserved. *E. C. Bennett and Martin Jenkins / Online Transport Archive*

Centre Other ex-Paisley cars found their way into Glasgow's large works-car fleet, which had its own base in Barrland Street (again close to Coplawhill works). These vehicles hardly ever ventured out in daylight hours, making this view of 27 (formerly 1005) particularly rare. The car is at Mosspark terminus on 21 February 1960. Note the mound of coal needed to fire the Permanent Way Department's tar boilers. Boiling tar was used for grouting between the granite setts. *E. C. Bennett and Martin Jenkins / Online Transport Archive)*

Beyond the Boundary
Among routes to close during the purges of the late 1950s were those that went miles beyond the city boundary, some of which ran by fields and down narrow country roads. On 23 May 1955, 'Cunarder' 1302 speeds along the former Paisley District private tramway laid between Darnley and Thornliebank in 1910. This was once part of the UK's longest tram route, covering a distance of more than 22 miles between Renfrew Ferry and Milngavie. Latterly, riding a four-wheeled 'Standard' on deteriorating permanent way could be something of a white-knuckle ride, and there are reports of one such tram losing the glass from its vestibule framing while travelling over a particularly rough section of track. This semi-rural area has since been developed.
Ray DeGroote / Online Transport Archive

Above In the autumn of 1956, a 'Hex-dash Standard' turns from Hope Street into Argyle Street to enter the 'Hielanman's Umbrella' — the large covered area beneath Glasgow Central station. Until 1957 this was a major tramway intersection with cars to and from George V Bridge crossing in the foreground. Today the roadway beneath the station is better lit but polluted by traffic flows. *Ray Bicknese / Online Transport Archive*

Above One memorable feature of the Glasgow system was all-female crews, and this charming study was taken in September 1959. There were many characters among the platform staff and it was once said they were auditioned for the job rather than interviewed. *Roy Hubble, courtesy LCC Tramways Trust*

Left The Glasgow tramway staff all rallied to ensure the service kept running when 50 cars were destroyed by fire at Dalmarnock depot on 22 March 1961. Fortunately, depot fires on tramways were relatively rare and were usually caused by a volatile cocktail of oil, wood, electricity and dust coupled with human error. The Dalmarnock conflagration was the last major tramway fire in the UK. Despite the loss no buses were used as substitutes. Vehicles were transferred or run from other depots, and a handful of cars withdrawn for scrap or preservation were returned to service thus extending the lives of the last 'Standards' and 'Kilmarnock Bogies' by a couple of months. But for a firewall, the intensity of the blaze would have consumed the northern half of the depot as well. *Harry Luff / Online Transport Archive*

Sauchiehall Street
Once the city's premier shopping thoroughfare, Sauchiehall Street has since lost this mantle to Buchanan Street. In happier times 1393 negotiates the busy junction with Hope Street on former 'yellow' service 24 to Langside. The little-used curves in the foreground were there for emergencies and diversions; when they were used it was not uncommon for trams to derail, although 'Standards' could usually cope with anything. The Gaumont cinema, home to long-running movies such as South Pacific and The Sound of Music, is now an indoor market. No 1393 was one of six 'Coronations' built in 1954 and mounted on bogies salvaged from a depot fire in Liverpool in 1947. *W. J. Wyse / LRTA (London Area)*

In addition to the mouth-wateringly high frequency all-day services enjoyed in Glasgow, the Corporation provided many additional trams or 'specials' to serve heavy industries both north and south of the Clyde. These were often worked by depots having no routine involvement in the services or the routes traversed. This line of cars of outbound cars are on Dumbarton Road on their way assist with the homeward exodus from the Clydebank shipyards in May 1955. The Coronation tram is being followed by no less than five 'Standards'. *Ray DeGroote / Online Transport Archive*

Glasgow used to employ ornate centre traction poles on a number of principal thoroughfares but they were found to impede traffic flows. Latterly, they only survived in two locations: the wide expanse of Shields Road and, here, on Glasgow Bridge, with its one-time intense tram service bringing people into the city from the southern suburbs. On his visit to Glasgow in May 1955, Ray DeGroote took several scenes on the bridge including this rare colour view of prototype five-window Coronation 1142 (left) on one of its rush hour sorties from Newlands depot. One-off cars like this were rarely popular in Glasgow because they were unfamiliar to crews. *Ray DeGroote / Online Transport Archive*

The Grand Finale

With each tramway closure the attendant ceremonies became ever more elaborate, culminating with a great Glasgow spectacle of 4 September 1962 when a grand cavalcade, representing different epochs, passed through streets lined with some 250,000 people. Not to be out done, the Burgh of Clydebank held its own last run two days later! Towards the end of the final ceremonial run on 4 September, magnificently restored 'Room & Kitchen' car 672 of 1898 makes its way through pouring rain to Coplawhill. This veteran is now on display at Glasgow's Riverside Museum.
E. C. Bennett and Martin Jenkins / Online Transport Archive

BLACKPOOL

- First street tramway in England, 1885
- Originally conduit operated
- Blackpool & Fleetwood Company acquired in 1920
- Massive modernisation programme started in 1933
- Lytham St Annes trams stop running into Blackpool in 1937
- Motor car and trailer set introduced in 1958
- Veteran trams restored for the 75th anniversary in 1960
- All other routes but the Promenade line closed between 1961-1963
- World's largest fleet of illuminated trams

The standard gauge Blackpool tramway is the great survivor. During the period covered by this book many changes were made and several routes were closed. During the 1950s, some of the 55 'Standards' built during the 1920s were still in evidence. Although their use on scheduled duties ended during the early 1950s, dwindling numbers still appeared as extras on the Promenade services until 1966. These big 78 seat cars on their Preston McGuire equal wheel bogies proved extremely useful absorbing the huge crowds which opted to tour the illuminations by tram. At the rear of this line up taken in October 1958 is No 41 which was scrapped following an accident in 1960. After the war, the Standards were the only non-air brake cars in the fleet. Several still survive. *Paul de Beer / Online Transport Archive*

Entering service during the 1920s, the 'Standards' were a mix of new and reconstructed cars, the latter incorporating parts and equipment from older vehicles. All eventually received vestibules and some became totally-enclosed although No 40, seen at Starr Gate in 1957, always retained its open balcony. It is on a section of track which had lain dormant for 20 years but was reactivated for use by a new Circular Tour only to close again in October 1961. The tracks to the left were used by Lytham St Annes trams until 1937. No 40 still survives today. *W.G.S Hyde / Online Transport Archive*

Built by Dick, Kerr of Preston the 48 seat 'Pantograph' cars (167-176) were so called because when delivered during 1928 to 1929 they had small towers supporting a pantograph, later replaced by conventional trolleypoles. Throughout their life, these 'Pullmans' operated almost exclusively between North Station and Fleetwood along the former interurban-style Blackpool & Fleetwood Tramroad (B&F) acquired by the Corporation in 1919. This was the only Blackpool service to be allocated a route number. Over the years the 'Pantographs' received various modifications and most, including 173 seen in Fleetwood, were given cascaded English Electric trucks during 1951 and 1952. Although the last examples were withdrawn from passenger service in the early 1960s, several survive today in various guises. *Everett White / Online Transport Archive*

Above A remarkable modernisation programme spearheaded by General Manager, Walter Luff, led to the purchase of 116 centre-entrance, streamline trams with English Electric bodies and trucks during 1933-1939. Among the new cars were 12 open 'boats' (225-236) delivered during 1934 and 1935 and intended for seasonal use on the Prom. These modern 'toastracks' had wooden slatted seats for 56 and two 40hp motors. 'Little Willy' (225), seen here on 9 April 1958, differed from the others in having lower sides. At the end of the 1950s, all 12 were fitted with driver's windscreens. Several still survive today. To the right is one of the legendary 'Balloons'. From 1955, the twin indicators on these cars were gradually replaced by a single display. *Phil Tatt / Online Transport Archive*

Opposite top In moves to adopt more modern technology, railcoach 208 played a significant role in 1946 when it was fitted with Vambac control equipment and the ceiling was lowered to accommodate the multi-notch accelerator located above the centre-entrance. At the same time, it was given new trucks, motors and braking. As a result, it became the forerunner of the later fleet of Marton Vambac cars. Here it prepares to run into Marton depot shortly before it was withdrawn in 1962. *E. C. Bennett and Martin Jenkins / Online Transport Archive*

Opposite bottom Some of the high-capacity 'Balloons' still form part of the current Blackpool fleet. Entering service during 1934 and 1935, they came in two distinct batches. 237-249 were designed as modern 'open-toppers' but with the possibility of closing off the upper deck during inclement weather. During 1941 and 1942, they were fitted with top covers similar to those on the 14 totally-enclosed Balloons (250-263). This reduced the former open-toppers overall capacity from 94 to 84 although some subsequently again held 94. In its war-time green and cream livery, 238 takes its layover at Lytham Road in 1952. The Lytham Road and South Pier sections were abandoned in October 1961. *B. C. Sexton / National Tramway Museum*

Included amongst the 116 new cars ordered by Walter Luff were the state-of-the-art Railcoaches. Following delivery of a striking prototype in 1933 a further 44 were delivered in two groups in 1933 and 1935 respectively. These 'luxury' cars were extremely comfortable with 24 upholstered seats in each saloon, floor heaters, sliding sunshine roofs, folding platform doors and separate driver's cabs. During the early 1960s, all but one of the 1933 Series 1 Railcoaches (200-224) were withdrawn. Then starting in 1957, 10 of the 1935 Series 2 Railcoaches (264-283) were transformed as part of a motor car and trailer programme whilst the remainder continued in service for many years. This Railcoach, still in the older green and cream livery, is seen at North Station in the early 1950s prior to making the run along the tramroad to Fleetwood. *W.J. Wyse / LRTA (London Area)*

In 1923, English Electric had supplied a very different vehicle to Blackpool. This was one of only a handful of steeple cabs operated on a British tramway. With its two 57hp motors this four-wheeler was used on the tramroad from 1925 to 1949 to haul coal wagons from Copse Road depot (seen here) to Thornton Gate sidings. At the rear of the depot was a connection onto the mainline railway. On 16 May 1955, it was about to depart with a short permanent way train. Today it is preserved at the National Tramway Museum. *Ray DeGroote/Online Transport Archive*

Not included in the 116 streamliners were 20 improved 'Railcoaches' (284-303) built by Brush in 1937 and mounted on EMB hornless bogies. On 16 May 1955, 287 stands outside the old North Station. This street track section as far as Gynn Square was abandoned in October 1963. Between 1958 and 1962, the twin indicators on most of the Brush cars were replaced by single displays. After being converted into a Vambac car, 303 was scrapped as 'non-standard' in 1963 but several of these Brush cars eventually clocked up nearly 75 years of service.
Ray DeGroote / Online Transport Archive

The last of Walter Luff's 116 English Electric cars were the 12 'sun saloons' (10-21) of 1939. Intended for summer use only, they were built on the cheap with recycled equipment, half-glazed windows, wooden seats, no driver's cabs, half-height doors and folding canvas roofs. During the war, proper glazing and full height doors were installed and the cars became crush-loaders nicknamed 'cattle trucks'. Then from 1948 to 1952 these 'ugly ducklings' were transformed into stylish modern cars with Crompton Parkinson Vambac equipment, Maley & Taunton HS44 trucks, driver's cabs, upholstered seats and fluorescent lights. Until 1962, they were the mainstay of the suburban Marton route. On 16 May 1955, No 16 is using the trolley reverser at Royal Oak terminus.
Ray DeGroote / Online Transport Archive

Walter Luff's final group of centre-entrance cars were the 25 'Coronations' of 1952 to 1954. Built by Charles Roberts, these 50ft long, 8ft wide cars had 56 comfortable seats, separate driver's cabs, glass panelled roofs, fluorescent lights, electro-pneumatic sliding doors, sliding standee windows, eye-catching interior fittings and the same basic equipment as the Marton Vambacs. Although popular with passengers and staff, (who nicknamed them 'Spivs'), these smooth running cars with their swift acceleration proved an increasing liability. They were costly to operate and maintain and the bodies suffered from water ingress. On some the troublesome Vambac equipment was eventually replaced by conventional equipment from older cars. The last examples were withdrawn in 1975. Three still survive. The once-familiar Blackpool style tram shelters (left) have long since been replaced. *Ray DeGroote / Online Transport Archive*

To increase capacity on the Promenade, English Electric Railcoaches 276 and 275 were reconstructed as a motorcar and trailer set. This view was taken on the inaugural day of operation – 9 April 1958 – when the virtually all-cream set was operating a Limited Stop Coastal Tour. Rebuilt to resemble the 'Coronations' they had electro-pneumatic folding platform doors and Willison couplers at each end. Eventually, a further eight English Electric Railcoaches were remodelled in similar fashion. When 10 new trailer cars built by Metropolitan Cammell-Weymann were delivered during 1960-61, 275 was rebuilt as a motor car. The last of these coupled sets was withdrawn in 2011.
Phil Tatt / Online Transport Archive

Between 1961 and 1963 all non-Promenade services were abandoned. Probably the most significant loss occurred in October 1962 with closure of the Marton route which served the town's residential hinterland. However, with one-man buses offering considerable savings, the running of crew-operated, 48-seat cars was no longer seen as financially viable. With only months to go a Marton Vambac purrs along Whitegate Drive. Historically, this was the last traditional all-street track tramway in the British Isles. After this spate of closures, even the long-term future of the world-famous Promenade tramway remained in doubt during the 1960s. *E. C. Bennett / Online Transport Archive*

Today, Blackpool still has a small fleet of illuminated cars but, over the years, old favourites have been scrapped or have left for pastures new. In 1959, two Standards, 158 and 159 of 1927, joined the illuminated fleet. During the Autumn Illuminations, the brightly lit cars carried passengers on evening tours of the illuminations; at other times, without their lights switched on, they were available for other duties. This arrangement continued until 1966. One of the pair is seen at North Station in October 1963 shortly before the North Station to Gynn Square section was abandoned. *E. J. McWatt / Online Transport Archive*

One of the other illuminated cars no longer with us is the lifeboat 'Jubilee'. Dating from 1926, it used parts from an old passenger car and was so named because it was launched on the occasion of Blackpool Borough's 50th anniversary. It is seen here at Bispham during its final season on 26 August 1961. *E. J. McWatt / Online Transport Archive*

The Blackpool fleet included a fascinating collection of non-passenger cars. In 1957, two long disused open toastracks were converted to carry TV cameras enabling outside broadcast units to bring the illuminations to a wider audience. One of the converted 'racks' No 166 is seen adjacent to the works in 1963. *E. J. McWatt / Online Transport Archive*

To mark 75 years of tramway operation in 1960, General Manager JC Franklin felt it would be appropriate to restore a number of vintage trams. One of those involved was the former B&F Box Car No 40 of 1914. Here it is seen prior to its restoration at Rigby Road depot in April 1958. *Phil Tatt / Online Transport Archive*